Times of Our Lives

D0332702

The Daily Telegraph

Times of Our Lives

Michael Oke

howtobooks

KENT ARTS & LIBRARIES		
C 152289776		
Askews		

Published by How To Books Ltd,
3 Newtec Place, Magdalen Road,
Oxford OX4 1RE. United Kingdom.
Tel: (01865) 793806. Fax: (01865) 248780
email: info@howtobooks.co.uk
www.howtobooks.co.uk

All rights reserved. No part of this work may be reproduced or stored in an information retrieval system (other than for purposes of review) without the express permission of the publisher in writing.

© Copyright 2004 Michael Oke

British Library Cataloguing in Publication Data.
A catalogue record for this book is available from the British Library.

Produced for How To Books by Deer Park Productions, Tavistock
Cover design by Baseline Arts Ltd, Oxford
Typesetting and design by Sparks – www.sparks.co.uk
Printed and bound in Great Britain by Bell & Bain Ltd, Glasgow

NOTE: The material contained in this book is set out in good faith for general guidance and no liability can be accepted for loss or expense incurred as a result of relying in particular circumstances on statements made in this book. Laws and regulations are complex and liable to change, and readers should check the current position with the relevant authorities before making personal arrangements.

Every effort has been made to identify and acknowledge the sources of the material quoted throughout this book. The author and publishers apologise for any errors or omissions, and would be grateful to be notified of any corrections that should appear in any reprint or new edition.

To my darling girls Mychelle and Katie, to my wonderful parents, and to the many friends who have trusted me to assist with their life stories, without whom this book would not have been possible.

Contents

How to Use This Book

This book is intended for those wishing to write their life story. It is aimed primarily at anyone born before the end of the Second World War, but the techniques used will also be of value to those of a younger vintage.

The emphasis is not to write a bestseller, but a personal record for family and friends to enjoy. Whilst those with higher ambitions will find the book helpful, it is essentially intended for the enthusiastic hobbyist writing to celebrate life. Typically this will include those you have known and loved, the events that have shaped your life, and the fascinating social history witnessed along the way.

Adopting a chronological approach, each chapter looks at a different aspect of life. Two chapters are devoted to the war years; which one is relevant will depend on your age. As with the rest of the chapters, feel free to pick and chose as appropriate. At the end of each chapter some writing tips are included, as well as questions to help stimulate further thought.

A series of personal anecdotes appear throughout the book, providing snap-shots of life in the middle years of the twentieth century – all are written by amateur authors who grew up in Britain during this era.

Finally, history notes covering the 50 years from 1930 are also included. In addition to national and world events, these include musical hits of the year, films, best-selling books and sporting highlights to further jog your memory.

Use this book as it suits you. Select what you want and let the memories roll!

Meeting the Family

1

This chapter looks at those who were likely to have been influential in your formative years – grandparents, parents, aunts, uncles and siblings. It also provides the opportunity to record what you know about those family members you were too young to remember; people who will live on through your book.

Making a start

The two most popular ways to start writing about your family are:

- ✎ introducing yourself;
- ✎ recording your family background.

Which you choose will depend, in part, on how much is known about the family history.

Introducing yourself

The easiest and most popular way to start your book is to introduce yourself and a few basic facts:

- your full name;
- your date of birth;
- where you were born;
- the names of your parents;
- brief details of other siblings;
- anything interesting about your birth.

The beauty of this straightforward approach is that it gets you into the swing of writing immediately.

Case study – Ann Davies

I came into this world at Burghclere, Hampshire, on 12 February 1936, the fifth child and third daughter of Harry and Caroline Hiller. Ahead of me were Mary, Leslie, Peter and Edith – Edith was known to us all as Queenie. I was christened Ann and for some reason was the only child to have just one forename – I thought that perhaps my parents had run out of names!

Home was a small council house – No.2 Harts Cottages – in a group of three semi-detached houses. I do not recall living there, as a couple of years later we moved house. However, this was no great upheaval as we moved next door to No.1. The reason for this minor migration was that our new home, being on the end of the block, was larger; it also had the bonus of a bigger garden.

(The story then carries on in this style with the introduction of Ann's three younger sisters. Details about grandparents, uncles and aunts are also gently incorporated into the story.)

Reflecting back

With the above approach, if you want to include some family history, you can introduce yourself and your immediate family and then write something like: 'Before I proceed too far with my own story, I will record a little of what I know about my ancestors.' This then provides an opportunity to write about those you never knew or were too young to remember.

Using flashbacks

If you do not have much information about your family background, you can include what you do know via a series of flashbacks, for example, '… my parents always went to the Lake District for their anniversary because that was where they met on a walking holiday and it always remained a special place for them.'

Recording your family background

Whatever information you know about your family background is worth including in your book. Starting from as far back as you can, even if it is only your grandparents, bring your writing up to the point where you enter the story. There is no need to undertake detailed genealogical research; just record what you know already. Snippets of information gleaned over the years might include:

- where the family originated;
- the derivation of the surname and any changes made over the years;
- family names and nicknames passed down the generations;
- the size of families;
- notable characters;
- recurrent careers and jobs;
- physical attributes passed down the generations;
- property owned by the family, or even an ancestral home.

You may well know more about your family background than you give yourself credit for. Not only will this be useful for setting the scene, but any future genealogists in the family will certainly be grateful as well. Relatives and family friends might also be able to provide additional detail.

Skeletons in the cupboard

If the 'skeletons' relate to relatively recent events, care should be taken in deciding what is included; it is not the intention here to open up old wounds or cause a family rift. However, where sufficient time has passed, don't miss the opportunity to include the stories that have gone down in family folklore.

Advice for genealogists

Those going back two or more generations might want to divide the material into the maternal and paternal sides of the family, including sub-headings for various branches of the family.

Whilst it is possible to include several chapters of family history alongside your own life story, care should be taken not to confuse the two projects. Genealogy can be a little on the dry side for those who are not so enthusiastic about the subject – even those within the family. Your life story, on the other hand, will appeal to a wider audience of family and friends alike, because it is about you – someone they know personally. Also, you will be able to include insights, feelings and anecdotes to bring your writing alive, something not easily achieved with the historical review.

Should you wish to include reams of information about your ancestors, several options exist:

- Use an appendix – Appendices are ideal for detailed and/or lengthy information which otherwise might create an imbalance in the book, putting off all but the most dedicated readers before they even reach the point where you are introduced to the story. The more pertinent information can be included at the beginning of the book with a reference to the full account in the appendix for those who are interested.

- Include tables and lists – Genealogical information can be concisely displayed in tables or lists, saving on pages of narrative. It is also easier to spot trends, like recurrent names and professions, by such presentation. If there are several pages, again, the best place may be the appendix.

- Keep additional information with the book – Storing your autobiography in a presentation box will keep it in pristine condition as well as being an ideal depository for information too voluminous even for an appendix.

- Insert a family tree – Reams of names and dates can be tedious when writing about distant ancestors. If these are displayed in a family tree, the more pertinent conclusions can then be included in the narrative without boring the reader. For example, 'My great-grandmother, Grace Gammon, was born on 3 October 1883. She was the third of 13 children, but as she had two older brothers it fell to her to look after the rest of the clan ….'

  If the family tree can be condensed onto a page or a folded larger sheet, it can be incorporated within the book perhaps as an appendix. Other options are to insert it into a wallet attached to the front or back inside covers of the book, or alongside the book in its presentation box. The advantage of keeping the family tree loose is that it can be updated as the family evolves.

- Redefine the project – You might have enough information to divide your book into two parts: one for recording your family history and the other for writing about your own life. This way your readers have the option of being selective and choosing what is of interest. The division can be explained in the introduction, and even reflected in the title of the book – 'The Life Story of George Lloyd, incorporating the History of the Lloyd Family'.

- Separate the book into two projects – If there is enough information for a book on family history alone, consider presenting this independently of your life story.

Beware the genealogy trap

If you decide to write your family history and your life story, it is advisable to start with your story as this is something only you can do – family records are still likely to be around at a later date for either you or someone else to investigate. Additionally, genealogy can become all-consuming, with one branch of research invariably leading to several more. Consequently, if you undertake this project first, you might never get round to writing your own life story!

Writing about parents and grandparents

This section is about those older members of the family who played such a large part in your early life. Whether it is parents, grandparents, aunts and uncles, or perhaps even a guardian, these are the people who influenced you and helped shape the person you have become. The danger is to assume that others know them as well as you do and not include as much information as you might.

A starting point is to describe appearances and personalities:

- what they looked like – height, size, colour of hair, etc. – and any distinguishing features;
- what they usually wore for work and in the home (possibly the same);
- their personality and any endearing qualities or peculiar mannerisms;
- their sense of humour, especially as shown through any anecdotes;
- the sound of their voice, any accent and how they spoke: for example, gently, with a soft Berkshire burr or no-nonsense plain talking;
- what appealed to you most about them;
- any favourite sayings, or their first words on entering the house;
- what they were called by family, friends and by you, and any pet names they had for you;
- possibly even how they spoiled you – or perhaps they were strict and you were a bit frightened of them.

Having provided this general overview consider:

- what gave them the greatest pleasure;
- what were their pet hates;
- their hobbies;
- their talents;
- the newspapers they read;
- their routines – like Dad coming in from work, removing his tie, putting his slippers on and sitting in his armchair in front of the fire reading his newspaper;
- what cigarettes or tobacco they smoked;
- what drinks they favoured;
- favourite authors and books, film stars and films, singers and songs, etc.;
- what sports they followed and their favourite teams and heroes;
- any family jokes associated with them.

If possible, try to include an anecdote to illustrate a point. For example, rather than saying that Gran was never lost for words, Iris Mechen included this account about her grandmother, Florence Brooker, who was being interviewed for a job in service at the age of 11.

Case study – Iris Mechen

Madam was about to dismiss Florence when she seemed to have an afterthought. 'Lift up your skirt, Florence,' she requested. 'I want to see if you are wearing knickers. A lot of girls arrive here without this vital undergarment and then complain of catching colds and chills, wanting time off work and expecting to receive their full pay, which is most unsatisfactory.'

Florence did as she was bid, saying, 'Yes Ma'am, I am wearing knickers, nice fleecy-lined ones that Mum got from an old lady who died in the village. Mum helped lay her out, so the relatives gave Mum a bundle of clothes to take home. I got the knickers and black stockings. They are a bit big, but I've folded them over at the top.'

This is your opportunity to preserve for posterity the memories of some of the most important people in your life. There are unlikely to be many people who remember them as well as you do, and what is not recorded will be lost forever.

Case study – June Brandon

Dad always found time for us girls if we were in the garden whilst he was working. He would give us rides in the wheelbarrow, or squirt water over us if he was watering the garden. As the cold spray splashed over us, we would squeal in mock anger, but really we loved it. He taught us how to dig a patch of earth and how to set seeds. He also showed us how to feed the chickens and how to be kind to animals. He loved his children and we loved him.

For the select few, you can include a review of their life at the point in your story when they die, possibly concluding the piece with a favourite photo of them.

Writing about siblings

Whilst older siblings are likely to be written about when introducing yourself, this need not be the case for younger brothers and sisters, particularly if you were old enough to remember their births – they can be introduced at that point in the story when they appeared.

It is useful to draw any patterns to the reader's attention, like the fact that there were three years between each of the five children, which tied in with your father's period of leave from his work in India. Or perhaps there were effectively two families within the family – yourself and your older sister, and then a gap of seven years before the next two were born. If you know why there was such a gap, include it. These patterns will be obvious to you, but will not necessarily be so to those reading your book.

You can write about your siblings throughout the book, including them at appropriate points in your story, or more exhaustively in one or two passages. If you prefer the latter approach, it might be worth at least two sections – the early years and then later in life – otherwise you might have married your brother off and introduced his three children and seven grandchildren before you have even started writing about your own schooldays!

Your writing about any siblings should include the same sort of detail as considered above for your parents, and don't pass up the opportunity for a good story.

Case study – Lil Fulker

One day as I was doing a jigsaw, Iris, standing beside me, was gesticulating about something and knocked Mum's treasured vase off the dresser. As it smashed on the floor, Iris leapt backwards in fright, and by the time Mum came in she was on the other side of the room and I was the one nearest to the broken vase. Mum jumped to the obvious conclusion that I was responsible and started smacking me, which to my warped sense of humour was funny as I was innocent. My laughter only goaded Mum, and the more she smacked the more I laughed, and the more I laughed the angrier she became. I laughed so much that I could not even protest my innocence. I guess it made up for the times I got away with it when I was guilty!

There were probably times when you were also at fault and this is your opportunity to put the record straight.

Case study – Sylvia Culverhouse

One day when Jean was particularly annoying me, Dad issued her with a warning that if she so much as touched me again she would be for it. Of course this was quite a challenge for Jean, and she touched me very very lightly on the arm with her finger. I yelled out. She ran down the road, hotly pursued by Dad who caught her just outside Mr Ayling's cottage, dragged her home and gave her a good hiding. I felt so guilty about this and have apologised to her over the years, as that good hiding was not deserved. So here it is in writing – sorry Jean!

Points to ponder

- Decide how you are going to start your book.
- Write a list of ten earliest memories.
- How would you like those who were important to you in your formative years to be remembered?
- Who were the three most influential people in your early life and what did you most admire about them?

Top tips

- As the most difficult part of writing a book is getting started, just write about anything that inspires you – your grandparents, your first day at school, or even when you retired. The order of the book can be sorted out later, and just because it will ultimately read chronologically, it doesn't have to be written that way.

- If writing in longhand or using a typewriter, loose-leaf A4 paper and a lever-arch file will help you organise your manuscript, rearranging the order as necessary as new memories arise. For those using a dedicated word-processor or computer, inserting new information is easily accommodated.

Childhood Home 2

This chapter reviews the childhood home of your formative years, probably from the ages of about 5 to 14. Obviously, any earlier memories should also be included, especially if they feature a different home. Even if such recollections are only glimpses or feelings, if they have remained with you over the years, why not share them with your readers?

If you had several different homes, concentrate primarily on the one or two that hold the most vivid memories. The significant differences of any other homes can then be compared to provide a contrast. This will be of particular interest if there was a move to another part of the country, or even abroad, as cultural and climatic differences may have brought about a whole new dimension to your life.

The childhood home holds a significant place in shaping your formative years, and as such warrants special attention in the writing of your life story. How much detail you include in your writing is a choice only you can make, but you are likely to be amazed at what you remember, so be prepared for an avalanche! For those who grew up during the war, this chapter should be considered in conjunction with Chapter 7, The War Years – Part I.

Describing the house

A useful way to recall the home of your childhood is to close your eyes and try to picture it in detail. If the home is still in the family, describing the size and layout will be easy, but it might also be worth visualising how it was in your childhood because it is likely that furniture, pictures, lighting, etc. will have changed significantly since that time.

Start off by providing an overview of your home, be it a two-up, two-down terraced house, a church manse, a rambling children's home, a tenement block, a tied cottage, a stately home, a council house, a flat, a caravan, a farmhouse, a 'prefab' or something else. It may be that the home was shared with a business, perhaps a shop; if this was the case, it is worth explaining how everything fitted together.

First impressions of the external appearance may provide a clue as to what was found inside, for example, a sparkling brass knocker polished daily and a washed doorstep edged with donkey stone is likely to reveal an equally spotless home … an overgrown garden will tell another story. Alternatively, the dull grey stone may have made the winters seem interminable, the red brick welcoming, or the pebbledash very up-market. The roof might even reveal its own story if the thatch caught fire or the slates were home to generations of starlings.

Wandering round the home

Having described the property, in your mind's eye enter through the door you usually used – possibly the back door. Perhaps you can even recall the handle and latch, and the colour and style of the door. If it was always left unlocked, say so … current generations will be amazed. If the door was usually locked, say where the spare key was kept – on a piece of string through the letterbox, under the doormat, or perhaps you kept one tied around your neck?

Even these simple details will help to bring memories flooding back. Perhaps you can hear the creak of the door, or maybe describe a particular smell … but not too graphically if the back door was next to the outside toilet! On entering the house the delicious aroma of cooking may have met you, and if you had a dog perhaps you were welcomed by a bounding hound. You might even be able to remember what you usually said, 'I'm home,' 'What's for tea?' or 'Is the kettle on, Mother?'

If you entered the kitchen or scullery, describe that first, or perhaps the hall if you came in through the front door. Start with the layout of the ground floor and then take a look at each room in detail.

The kitchen

The kitchen is likely to have been one of the most significant parts of the home, especially if it also contained the living area. Not only was the warmth of the range or cooker important but before the advent of modern labour-saving devices it was also where your mother will have spent most of her time. You might like to start by describing the smell that hit you:

- freshly-baked bread;
- the smoky fire;
- the stew or soup that your mother invariably had on the go;
- bleach, which seemed to be used all the time;
- the dampness of drying clothes on a wet Monday afternoon;
- mothballs;
- goose grease, if someone had a cold.

Go on to describe the main characteristics of the kitchen, and possibly any adjoining scullery or pantry:

- the size and layout;
- the décor … even if it was only distemper;
- the different doorways leading off;
- what was on the ceiling? – A Dutch airer, sticky fly papers, etc.;
- what was on the floor? – Paving slabs, lino (fitted wall-to-wall?),

coconut mats, rag rugs, Congoleum (squares of lino, patterned to look like carpet).

Not only will these details provide a fascinating social history, there may also be some associated stories.

Case study – Joy Kennedy

The kitchen was a cosy room at the back of the house where I spent many hours enjoying Gran's company while Mum coped with the little ones. There was a fire, which Gran banked up at night, and in the centre of the room was a table, white and well scrubbed, covered with a brownish chenille tablecloth if no baking was being done. In the corner was a cupboard under the stairs, my favourite place to play. When I think about it now I go cold as one of my games was to crawl down to the end of this cupboard and make a camp. I would then light a candle and toast cheese on a fork! There never was a fire, but it could easily have happened.

Perhaps you can recall what banking up the fire involved:

- larger lumps of coal on the remaining embers;
- nutty slack;
- peelings;
- perhaps even a sprinkling of water.

Then there were the various built-in features in the kitchen:

- the cooking range – describe it, how it was used and any idiosyncrasies;
- the copper, possibly with a wooden cover – perhaps you also washed yourself in the copper quite apart from its use on wash-day;
- the sink – whilst a butler sink is now considered trendy, it would not have been so in your childhood … especially if it was not plumbed in;
- the larder – not forgetting what was inside: the marble slab, milk

jug with beads hanging from the embroidered doily, the meat-safe, etc.

The furniture in the kitchen/living room is also sure to evoke some memories. Try to picture such things as:

- the mantelpiece, possibly with a runner with tassels or a lace adornment, and the various photos, ornaments and odds and ends kept on it;
- cupboards and their contents;
- a sideboard, and how it was looked after;
- the work surfaces your mother used, and what other makeshift areas she requisitioned for extra space;
- a Welsh dresser and the precious items displayed there;
- forbidden drawers and cupboards;
- the clock – whose job was it to wind it up?

It might help to try to remember what was kept where:

- cutlery;
- crockery;
- saucepans;
- tablecloths;
- cruets;
- sauces and pickles;
- soap, bicarbonate of soda and disinfectants;
- health remedies like Parish's Food, Beechams Pills ('worth a guinea a box') cod liver oil, syrup of figs, etc.;
- Dad's strop;
- the washboard and lading can;
- irons;
- Dad's pipe rack, tobacco pouch or cigarettes;
- ashtrays;
- pictures and photographs;
- ornaments and knick-knacks;
- the broom and dustpan and brush;
- a cane to remind you to behave;
- money tins for saving for the rent, the gas meter, the coalman, milkman, doctor, etc.;
- odds and ends like spare keys, string, pencils, old stamps, etc.;

     ⁅   anything strange – like Dad's bike;

     ⁅   as very few people had bank accounts, and there were certainly no credit cards, where was the money kept – behind the clock on the mantelpiece, in a teapot or caddy in a cupboard?

Certain items of furniture will demand greater attention:

     ⁅   The kitchen table – if the kitchen table could speak it would have an amazing story to tell – after all, it was used for so many things: ironing; dress-making; minor operations (on you or your pets); plucking chickens; doing homework (usually at the last minute); mending punctures; making jam, pastry, puddings and cakes; pickling everything; making wine; carving the meat; hiding under (especially if it was a Morrison table) ... oh yes, it was also used for eating on!

     ⁅   The chairs – perhaps there was a pecking order in your family and everyone had their own seat – if so, where was yours, and was there anything special about it? You might also like to describe where your parents sat, and what happened if you sat in their nice warm chair by the fire. Perhaps you can picture your father sitting in his armchair cleaning his pipe and tamping the tobacco ... even recalling the brand and the aroma, and when thinking about your mother, where would she be, what would she be doing and what would she be wearing?

The power supply

Describe the power supply – electricity, gas or oil, or was it coal fires, paraffin lamps and candles? Of course, you may have used several of these as some houses only had gas downstairs ... it cost more to be installed upstairs.

Coal fires may sound romantic, but there was little romance when it came to dealing with the soot and smoke, making the annual spring-clean a necessity. If sweeping the chimney, chopping wood, cleaning out the grate, playing with fire tongs, or even drying the washing on the fireguard, give rise to any interesting stories, you might like to include them.

Perhaps an overriding memory is how cold your home was, especially in winter, and the measures you took to get warm: leaving the oven door open, wearing several layers of clothes, putting your feet in the oven or keeping your coat on. And then of course there were the itchy and painful chilblains you got as a result of the temperature extremes and sitting too close to the fire – your shins roasting while the back of your legs froze.

If your remember gaslight, describe the delicate operation of lighting the mantles, whose job it was, and how easily they broke when touched. There might also have been a gas boiler with its various foibles and noises.

While some of the more sophisticated homes boasted electricity, this did not necessarily mean that there was an abundance of plug sockets – not that there were many labour-saving devices to utilise such advances. Using an electric iron may have meant removing the light bulb and plugging the lead into the light fitting in the ceiling.

'Modern' technology

Wireless

You may remember the excitement of getting your first wireless set. As this was a very expensive piece of equipment, the odds are that it was not to be touched by children … perhaps your only involvement was lugging the heavy accumulator battery to the garage to be recharged, trying to avoid spilling the acid in the process.

You might recall some interesting anecdotes, like your father listening to the football results every Saturday for the pools forecast, and having to keep very quiet. What was his favourite team, and how did he react if they won or lost?

Case study – Violet Kentsbeer

Our first wireless was a wonderful invention; it was called a crystal set and only Dad was allowed to touch it. I can see him now, tinkering with a little piece of wire attached to a holder. In the middle of the set the wire (cat's whisker) had to touch the crystal just in the right place, and hey presto you got a sound. Of course, you had to wear earphones to hear anything, but oh!, the excitement of hearing Uncle Mac saying, 'Hello children everywhere.' We had to take turns listening in, as there was only one pair of earphones and there were four of us waiting to have a go. When we moved, we went all posh and had a battery set.

Some will identify more readily with Ron Larkin:

Case study – Ron Larkin

We had a plug-in *Ultra* mains radio, as opposed to the one that ran off an accumulator – a glass-bodied battery-type contraption. The radio had three wavebands – long wave, medium wave and short wave – a long time before things like AM, FM and VHF frequencies. The dial from which you selected the station was a bit like a geography lesson, with names such as Helsinki, Sofia, Hilversum and Daventry. Having, at that time, no idea where these places were, I can remember spinning the knob at great speed, which resulted in foreign gibberish spewing out of the loudspeaker.

From the medium-wave band, you could listen to the BBC programmes. The BBC provided just three stations. The first was known as the 'Home Service', which catered for highbrow tastes and had classical music, serious plays, programmes like *The Brains Trust* and discussion programmes. The second station was the 'Forces Programme' – later to be renamed the Light Programme – and this contained news, popular music and programmes like *Music While You Work*. The third station was the BBC World Service, which was actually transmitted on short wave – the waveband for extreme ranges.

Telephone

Unless it was required for business, telephones were not common in most homes, and even then it often involved using the operator … who tended to know more information than was considered appropriate!

Case study – Douglas Badham

In the late 1930s, the telephone was only in its infancy and you could not just dial or press the numbers – indeed, there was not even a dial. When you picked up the receiver, an operator would ask what exchange number you wanted. If the number was engaged or unobtainable, the operator at the exchange in question would come on and explain the position to you. My parents' number was 'Hengoed 79' and I remember one occasion when the operator at Hengoed came on the line and said to me, 'I'm afraid I can't get a reply, but Mr Badham is usually playing bridge at Dr Davis' on a Saturday evening – shall I try there?'

The front room

In many instances the front room was only used on Sundays or when visitors came. It may seem strange for large families to limit the use of the house in this way, but at least it saved on heating costs. You might be able to remember such items as:

- treasured ornaments;
- vases;
- plush curtains;
- elaborate light fittings;
- a mirror and pictures on the wall;
- a piano;
- posh chairs with antimacassars;
- family photographs;
- cabinets displaying the best glasses and crockery;

    ❧ ashtrays on a stand;
    ❧ the newest rag rugs;
    ❧ an aspidistra on the table;
    ❧ dustcovers on the furniture!

If this room was used infrequently, think about some of the occasions when you were permitted to go in there:

    ❧ enduring visits from distant relations, sitting upright and only speaking when spoken to;
    ❧ listening to records on the gramophone;
    ❧ performing plays with your friends for the entertainment of the adults;
    ❧ reading quietly on Sunday afternoons as you were not allowed to play boisterous games, this being a day of rest;
    ❧ playing cards at Christmas, and Uncle Bert getting squiffy;
    ❧ joining in the family singalong by the piano;
    ❧ spying on your older sister, awkwardly entertaining her boy-friend;
    ❧ seeing your grandmother lying in her coffin.

The hall and stairs

If your home had these, such areas may trigger some interesting recollections:

    ❧ the mirror in the hall for checking your appearance before leaving the house;
    ❧ the table for messages – which was later used for the telephone, when you had one installed;
    ❧ the hat stand (because everyone wore a hat), and where you kept your shoes, boots, umbrellas …;
    ❧ a pram being kept in the hall, or perhaps a bike or two;
    ❧ a 'spear' behind the front door with a curtain on it – especially during the blackout;
    ❧ having to sit on the stairs when you were naughty, waiting for Dad to come home;

❧ playing cricket in the hall when your parents were out, and having to explain scuff marks on the back of the front door;

❧ the cupboard under the stairs where you played, or hid during the wartime bombing;

❧ the squeaky second stair which you had to avoid when sneaking home late at night;

❧ the joy of having carpet on the stairs ... but even then it was not fitted the whole width;

❧ you might even be able to remember exactly how many stairs there were!

Case study – Edward Stanley-Jones

I started at *Barkers* as a junior in the carpet department for £1 per week. Part of our work was to maintain a list of customers who wanted their carpets altered to spread the wear. Men were sent to these homes twice a year to remove the stair rods and move the carpets six inches or so. In this way the tread would now cover the vertical part of the stair, and the riser would become the tread, spreading the wear and extending the life of the carpet. Half a guinea (10s 6d – 52½p) was charged for each visit.

Upstairs

Having described the layout of the rooms upstairs, elaborate on your own bedroom, not forgetting to mention if you shared it with anyone. Stories might emerge from some of the ideas listed below:

❧ going to bed by candlelight if there was no other power source;

❧ being scared going upstairs in the dark, especially in the winter months ...;

❧ ... and being annoyed that you could hear your friends still playing outside on the long summer evenings when you had to be in bed by 7:30;

- ❧ the delights or otherwise of sharing a bed with siblings;
- ❧ keeping each other awake and the repercussions from your parents;
- ❧ pillow fights and the down going everywhere;
- ❧ reading under the bedcovers;
- ❧ the type of device used to warm the bed, for example, a hot water bottle, heated brick or hot shelf from the oven;
- ❧ waking up in the morning and seeing your breath in front of your face and ice on the inside of the windows;
- ❧ only having the fire lit if anyone was ill;
- ❧ if there was no bathroom upstairs, perhaps there was a jug of water and a basin in the room … and a 'guzzunder' (chamber pot) for emergencies during the night;
- ❧ possibly having nightmares, and the reception you received if you ran into your parents' bedroom;
- ❧ it might even be worth mentioning that a time before duvets existed, when blankets, sheets and eiderdowns were the norm.

Other areas of the house

Perhaps there was a special place where you played … legitimately or otherwise! Such areas might include an attic, a basement, your parents' bedroom, a nursery, a junk room, a large cupboard, or a flat roof outside your bedroom.

Decorating the house

If you were allowed to decorate the house, who would do this and are there any interesting stories relating to it? Perhaps it was a case of having to draw the curtains, whitewash the windows or cover them with newspaper so that the neighbours could not see in! If the landlord was responsible for decorating, describe the routine and what choice you had regarding the colour scheme.

The backyard

Having thoroughly toured the house, it is now time to go outside into the backyard. If you had an outside toilet, was it flushable, a hole cut in a piece of wood above a pit or bucket, or something in between? If there was a bucket or pit, say who had the unenviable task of emptying it, and where it was emptied … it may explain why the vegetable garden was so productive! Alternatively, a wagon may have come round periodically to remove the contents, evoking a few more memories.

Case study – Ken Baxter

The toilet was the vault type, on top of which was a big wooden board with a hole in it. Down the hole was a pit about 10ft deep, 6ft wide and 10ft long. Round the back, outside, was a trap door where the toilets were emptied. Occasionally we might be in the toilet and hear a cat mewing from below, understandably in a state of great distress as there was no way it could get out. We would run to tell Mum, then get the bucket on the long pole and try to scoop the cat through the trap door at the back. Once we had got it, we would throw an old sack over the poor creature and take it to Edie Hill, the lady who lived in the terrace who delivered the newspapers. For some reason she always cleaned the cats … rather her than me!

Some people may remember two or more sharing a toilet cubicle, or perhaps running down the street before bedtime in pyjamas or a nightie to a communal toilet block – something almost inconceivable nowadays. Of course, there might have been further horrors lurking in the form of spiders and other creepy-crawlies, and it was probably quite scary on a dark winter's evening, especially if there was no light. Then there were the newspaper squares on a piece of string for the toilet paper, and the dread of running out, especially if the loo was at the end the garden, out of earshot of someone who could come to the rescue … and whose job was it to ensure a ready supply?

Case study – Betty Grainger

Squares of old newspaper were strung together and then hung on a nail inside the toilet. Even then we had to be sparing as the size of newspapers was limited during the war. The person to use the last piece of paper had to tear up some more, however we tended to take our turn in doing this job.

Dad had *The Record* during the week, and *The Sunday Post* and *News of the World* on Sundays. The *News of the World* was for adults only and we children were forbidden to read it. Of course, once in squares for the toilet paper, our eyes would devour any juicy gossip and our stay in the loo would be longer than necessary.

Other things found in the backyard might include a mangle, a tin bath, a coal-shed or bunker, a washhouse, your father's work shed, a washing line, the dustbin and maybe a bicycle or two. Also, was the yard kept scrupulously clean, or was it a bit of a junk area?

The garden

Front and back gardens are also worth describing, whether they were wonderful play areas or more functional vegetable gardens. Perhaps flowers were your passion, and Dad's green fingers inspired you to cultivate your own plot of land, developing a lifelong interest. More extensive gardens may have meant keeping a few hens, buying them as day-old chicks. Explain how they were reared and fed, and whose job it was to collect the eggs. Perhaps there were even enough to store in isinglass. Then the time came for eating the hens – probably boilers, but maybe there was the occasional younger chicken for roasting, even if this was only at Christmas. Whose job was it to kill and pluck the birds, and what stories does this trigger?

Case study – Joan Belk

One Christmas I watched in horror as Dad took the hatchet across the spare ground to our allotment and put the tree stump ready. Then he proceeded to chase the hens round the garden, without much success … after about half an hour he eventually caught one. He raised the hatchet, but when I opened my eyes he hadn't done anything. He then called me over and said, 'Pidge, fetch the farmer's boy – everybody to their own job,' and with that he disappeared down the pub for a pint … it must have been thirsty work chasing hens around!

Don't forget to include any other livestock you kept, such as rabbits, and the qualms you felt when these were dished up on your dinner plate. The odd pig or two may also have been kept, especially during the war. If this was the case, how did they meet their end? Also, describe how the carcass was divided up and preserved. Maybe it was shared between neighbours, who reciprocated when their pig was slaughtered.

An allotment, shed, pigeon loft or some other place where your father loved to hide away is worth recording, along with any interesting stories that spring to mind. Those who lived on a smallholding or a farm will have much more to include. Describe the different types of livestock and crops farmed, also considering the various routines throughout the farming year. Also, with scant regard for health and safety matters, there are likely to be some stories about accidents and the dangers of farm life.

Wider research

Whilst none is necessary, more enthusiastic scribes can pursue some simple research.

Looking at photographs

Any photos taken at home are likely to show something in the background. Seeing the furniture, pictures on the wall, the décor, doors and windows, and even the garden might set some memories rolling. Any old ciné films will be better still.

Chatting to relations

Relations and friends who knew your childhood home can be a rich source of information. In addition to their own valuable recollections, the conversation is likely to stimulate further memories between you. Often these will be linked to an interesting anecdote, providing further material for your writing.

Visiting your old home

If your childhood home is still standing and not too far away, paying a visit is bound to stimulate some memories. Looking at the outside, even if it has changed substantially, will remind you of its general appearance, the dimensions, the garden and the geography in relation to other landmarks. It might even be possible to arrange for an internal viewing, especially if the new owner is interested in knowing a little of its history.

Contacting estate agents

If your home was one of many identical houses in a street, the odds are that a similar one (or its mirror image, if it was semi-detached) will be on the market sooner or later. Contacting an estate agent in that area and explaining your reasons will pay dividends when you receive particulars in the post. The dimensions of the rooms will help you to place furniture, and you might be amazed at how much smaller the house is than how you remembered it!

Points to ponder

-   Describe your feelings about your childhood home.
-   What was you favourite place in the house?
-   What are your most powerful memories of that house?

Top tips

-   Know how you work best; it might be 10 o'clock every morning with a cup of tea or sitting up in bed at 1:00 am. Whether you are a lark or an owl, write at those times of the day when you feel most relaxed and inspired.

-   If you are easily distracted, consider booking a date in your diary for writing, then if something else crops up you can legitimately claim that you are otherwise engaged. Alternatively, impose a deadline on yourself by telling a friend that you hope to send them your first chapter by the end of the month. Even this loose commitment will help focus your mind.

Neighbourhood

3

Having taken a look at your childhood home, this chapter uses similar techniques to review the area in which you lived. It is likely that the place of your birth and where you lived in childhood will be mentioned early on in your writing, when you introduce yourself in the story. That information can now be developed to provide the reader with an understanding of the place that shaped your early years, its characters and a way of life long since gone.

Whether you were brought up in Britain or abroad, the same attention to detail can be considered. Whilst the neighbourhood of your youth will be obvious to you, it will not be so for everyone. Younger readers will also need guidance if the area has changed extensively over the years.

If it is convenient, you might want to visit the place where you grew up, perhaps even asking around to see if there's anyone remaining from your childhood days. Any discussions will be fascinating and will provide even more material for your manuscript. Some photos of the area and your school can also be included in your book.

Providing a general overview

The sort of details to consider include:

- the name and character of the village or town, or the district within a city – industrial, rural, wealthy, deprived, cosmopolitan;
- if appropriate, the proximity to the nearest large town or city;
- the approximate size and/or population of the village/town/city;
- any dominant geographical features: hills, rivers, canals, proximity to the sea;
- communication links: main roads, railways, trams …;
- the principal industries and types of employment;
- if rural, the type and size of farms – for example smallholdings or tied farms;
- the predominant housing: properties tied to the local estate or industry, rented rooms, private houses, tenement blocks, etc.;
- the class structure (if you were aware of it), and the names of any local 'bigwigs'.

Drawing a plan of the area

Sketching a simple plan will help you remember a myriad of details. These might include:

- where friends lived;
- the shops, pubs, school, church, village hall …;
- where certain people lived: the doctor, policeman, vicar, midwife, etc.;
- local factories, farms, abattoir and so on;
- the gasworks – where you collected the coke … or perhaps a slag-heap where you nicked the coal;
- play areas, woods and fields;

   ℣ recreation ground and bandstand;

   ℣ the areas that were out-of-bounds to you … or so your parents thought!

Case study – Ken Baxter

The fair came to Stamford every year just before Easter, a tradition dating back a hundred or more years. The town would be at a standstill with most of the streets shut off so that the stalls and various rides could be set up. Janet and I had a great time at the fair that year. We went every night, and whilst it was heavy on the pocket, it was worth every penny. The hit song at the time was *Ghost Riders in the Sky* by Frankie Lane, and whenever I hear it I can picture those rides on the 'Cape Walk' where this song blared out non-stop. Nowadays, I believe that the fair is only about a quarter of the size as new laws and fire regulations dictate that the streets cannot be closed.

Obviously what is included on your plan will depend on where you lived. If this was a village you might know every nook and cranny, whilst those who lived in a large city are likely to have a detailed knowledge of the immediate area and only a sketchy acquaintance with places further afield. Those who lived in the middle of nowhere will have a different playground to describe, as well as explaining where the nearest amenities were and how they had to improvise as a result.

Including travel routes

On your plan of the area insert some of your regular journeys, maybe to school or to your grandparents' house. These might be on foot or bike, or perhaps involved a bus, train, tram or ferry ride … maybe even a car for the fortunate few.

Avoid missing the obvious

When describing the area, it is easy to overlook the obvious. Even living on a fruit farm in deepest Kent there are some things that need to be explained.

Case study – Don Buss

When I was seven we moved to 'Gasometer Cottage', Broadstairs, a strange name for a farmhouse in the middle of 50 acres of orchards in the Kent countryside. The apparent misnomer was soon explained when we saw a vast gasometer next to our new home. It consisted of a large supporting structure, some 20–30 ft deep, with the gas container rising to a dome in the middle. The gasometer had never been used, and as we had no gas or electricity in the house it seemed a strange place to find one, but apparently the railway had been expected to run close by, making it easy for the transportation of coal. Being snobs, we quickly changed the name to 'Orchard House'… considerably more refined we thought.

Taking the reader for a walk

Some people like to walk their reader around the area, pointing out the local landmarks and who lived where. Your plan of the neighbourhood will help with this and should spark memories of incidents and anecdotes associated with places, friends and neighbours. If you feel so inclined, you can even include a plan of the area in your book.

Character portraits

In writing about friends and neighbours, you might want to describe their characters and any distinguishing features, along with an anecdote or two if possible. Others who may also warrant attention include the policeman, local dignitaries, the pub landlord, or a snooty neighbour who objected to you scrumping apples. Don't forget the bully and anyone else you tried to avoid … or maybe you were the local bully! If strong feelings spring to mind about anyone – positive or negative – it is likely that an anecdote will be involved. Similarly, try to think of any embarrassing moments – they often remain as vivid as the day they occurred and invariably are connected with a good story … if you are brave enough to record them.

Case study – Lil Fulker

Jean Patterson is a name I cannot erase from my memory. It still evokes a feeling of guilt. The brooch she was wearing caught my interest. It was just a plain, gold brooch – in retrospect cheap gold-coloured metal – in the shape of a Scottie dog. I fell in love with it. Then at playtime, scuffing in the grass at the edge of the playground, I saw it gleaming up at me. I picked it up and pinned it to my dress, at once guilty and yet guileless. So engrossed was I in savouring the joy of wearing the coveted brooch that I was blissfully unaware that it was blatantly obvious to everyone what I had done.

My joy was short-lived! Almost before we had taken our seats Jean Patterson spotted the brooch. 'Miss, Miss, she's got my brooch!'

'Stand up Lily Goree. Is that your brooch you are wearing?'
'Yes, Miss.'
'Where did you get it?'
'My mum bought it for me in *Woolworths* on Saturday.'

The lie came so glibly to my lips that I did not recognise it for what it was. I believed it even as I said it.

'Right ... Thomas, go to Miss Rackstraw's class and fetch Mollie Goree, please.'

About a hundred years passed while I stood, the class whispering furtively. By now I so believed the lie that I was confident my sister would back me up, thus proving my innocence and enabling me to keep the brooch I prized so much. Alas no! She was obviously quite bewildered as to why I should lay claim to something that I knew perfectly well did not belong to me. 'No, I have never seen it before,' Mollie stated flatly.

Oh, the disgrace I felt! Yet even the public shame of surrendering the brooch, and the punishment of spending the remainder of the morning standing in the corner, was overshadowed by the disappointment of having to return it to its rightful owner. That is why 'Jean Patterson' and 'guilt' are indelibly printed on my heart forever!

The darker side of life

Many favourable aspects of community life will be recorded, but not everything should be viewed through rose-tinted glasses.

Case study – Violet Kentsbeer

Poverty, drink and gambling do not make very happy bed-fellows, and quite often a domestic row and fight would break out, and as most of the houses had been converted into flats, it was not unusual to see china and saucepans being thrown out of top windows. It was almost a form of entertainment; folk from other streets would come and watch to see what would happen in the end. Marriage guidance counselling – whatever was that? Families sorted out their problems as best they could.

What others thought of you

Critical opinions tend to be expressed more frequently than positive ones, so if you know what others thought of you or your family, it might not be of an uplifting nature. If you feel comfortable about recording such recollections, the reader may see a different side to your early life.

Tapping into the senses

Try to recall the smells associated with the area:

- sulphurous smog;
- freshly mown grass;
- farmyard odours;
- heavy industry;
- fragrant flowers;
- manure deposited in the road.

Case study – Violet Kentsbeer

Our neighbour delivered bread for *Clark's Bakery* by horse and cart, and when Mr Cordes came home for lunch the horse would stand outside our house wearing a nosebag. If we were lucky, the horse would leave behind a little surprise packet, if you know what I mean! This was very good for the garden and brought the roses on a treat. Dad, not being home during the day, would ask us to go out with a bucket and shovel and collect this free manure. I am afraid I was at the age – nearly 12 – when I thought it was below my dignity. Not so my sister Win, who usually got the job.

Similarly, there may be certain sounds associated with the area:

- the factory horn, by which you could set your watch (… at least you could if you possessed one);
- the regular running of trains or trams;
- the squealing of pigs being strung up in the abattoir;
- the knocker-upper who cost 1d a day;
- church bells, except during the war years when it was claxons, whistles, sirens, etc.;
- the cries of the various street traders.

Thinking laterally

It is also interesting trying to recall what was not around in your childhood. For example, if there were no streetlights, or lights of any sort, you may remember how dark it was. You may have been frightened by this, or perhaps marvelled at the brilliance of the stars in the dark night sky. Similarly, with far less traffic about, silence may have been a feature of your childhood – something you took for granted then, but rarely experience today.

Animals

Whether you lived in a town or in the country, the animals that featured in your childhood may provoke some anecdotes:

- the Shire horses pulling the brewery dray cart;
- the organ-grinder's monkey;
- a frightening bull in the field you were warned to avoid;
- the milkman's horse;
- the cows on the farm – all of which you knew by name;
- your pet dog, cat, chickens, mice ….

Case study – Peter Deeth

For many years we badgered Mother to let us have a dog, and finally we acquired a wonderful little red setter puppy, who was promptly Christened 'Barny' and thoroughly spoilt by all three children. Anyone who has owned a red setter knows what idiots they are – perfectly adorable, but not the brightest of God's creatures! I often took Barny for walks along Leigh cliffs, but as soon as I let him off the lead he was completely out of control. He would bound up to anyone and try to lick their face, and also had a dreadfully embarrassing habit of shoving his nose up unsuspecting ladies' skirts. As a young lad of 14 or so, I experienced some dreadfully embarrassing moments retrieving him and, with beetroot face, trying to apologise.

He once took himself down to Leigh Station and boarded a train to Fenchurch Street, London. There were several people in the carriage and everyone thought that the dog was with someone else. They eventually all got out at various stations on the way and the train steamed into Fenchurch Street with Barny all on his own, comfortably installed in a corner seat, looking out of the window. The startled porter rescued him, read the tag on his collar, and put him on the next train back to Leigh, this time with the guard in charge.

Shops

Few shops from childhood days will bear any similarity to those of today and so this is a ripe area for your book. With no fridges or freezers in the home, local shops and deliverymen were an essential part of everyday life – they were also part of the social fabric of the neighbourhood. The number and variety of shops you frequented will depend on where you lived, but select those of particular interest and that evoke special memories. Consider such things as:

- the location, appearance, name and type of shop;
- the smell and atmosphere;
- what was sold, and how it was displayed: tea, sugar, flour, butter, cheese, bacon, biscuits (broken ones being cheaper), sweets, etc.;
- how sugar, tea, butter, etc. were wrapped up, and the dexterity of the assistant in performing these tasks;
- the type of delivery system offered, if any;
- how the various products were arranged, for example, paraffin next to the bacon, and how the flies were kept away ... if they were;
- the form of address adopted by the shop staff/owner and the customers;
- the form of address adopted between the owner and any staff;
- how, as a child, you often had to wait because adults were always served first, even if they arrived after you;
- how payment was made, especially if it involved a system of wires across the ceiling;
- whether pins were ever given instead of a farthing change;
- what the system was regarding credit or 'tic';
- whether they accepted Provident Cheques;
- if it was a Co-op, what your mother's 'divi' number was;
- what you always coveted but could never afford.

Write about any special stories relating to getting the order wrong, being short-changed or perhaps losing the change on the way home and the repercussions that ensued. On a more positive note, describe the ritual when the 'divi' was paid out ... at least it made up for the tedium of having to count and collate all the vouchers.

Special treats also make for good reading, like eating chips out of the newspaper, especially if a few bits of batter were thrown in for good measure, or perhaps a bag of stale cakes the baker sold off cheaply.

Case study – Doreen Badham

My mother dealt with a high-class grocer called Cromwell Jones. She went once a week to do the shopping and, on entering the shop, a chair was brought, upon which she would sit while giving her order! When ordering bacon, the whole side was brought forth, 'How would you like it cut, Mrs Phillips? ... and what thickness would you like?' A massive block of butter was on view and an appropriate amount would be cut off, weighed then shaped into a neat square. To finish off, a swan was stamped into the butter! Biscuits were chosen from tins, each with a glass lid so the contents could be seen; biscuits were ordered by weight.

After giving her order, my mother would leave the shop, with the goods being delivered that evening and paid for quarterly. At Christmas time, Mr Jones enclosed a gift with the order ... either a bottle of *Johnny Walker* or a box of chocolates, as a 'thank-you' for the custom.

It is also interesting to view the workings of the shop from the other viewpoint.

Case study – Ken Baxter

At this time *International Stores* were a chain of good old-fashioned grocery shops. This was well before the advent of supermarkets, and the emphasis was always on good service. The customer really was king and his or her every need was our concern. Indeed, it was a sackable offence to talk to a colleague and ignore a customer, especially if that customer walked out without buying anything. After all, the *Co-op* was just over the road and they would be more than happy to poach any of our disgruntled customers.

There were two counters in the shop. All new staff started on the grocery counter where most of the goods were either in tins or jars. A couple of exceptions were tea-leaves and biscuits, both of which had to be weighed. The provisions counter was for the fresh produce, cooked meats, bacon, butter, cheese, lard, etc. More skill was required here and so new staff would only move to this counter once they had mastered all there was to know about the groceries.

There were two chairs in the shop, one in front of each counter, where the customers sat while their orders were made up. The assistant would write out a ticket, and the customer took this to the cashier to settle up. There were six or eight staff in the shop, and if it was not very busy an assistant would usually collect the whole order for the customer from both counters; some assistants looked after their own regulars.

A few customers were not above trying the occasional fiddle, and one of the senior staff would usually allocate a junior to watch them in case they tried anything suspicious. A favourite trick was to suddenly remember a minor item, like a half-pound of lard, after the main order had been made up. The customer would then go back and order the lard, receive a new ticket for a few pennies, go to the cashier and pay only this second smaller ticket before walking out with several pounds' worth of goods. We soon got wise to this and would shout to the cashier, 'Two tickets,' as the customer went to pay. Of course, it was always easy to double-check who the careless assistant had been because all tickets were written on a pad in duplicate and so two records were kept – on the counter and with the cashier. Woe betide us if we were taken for a ride.

Money

Whilst writing about shops, you might like to include something about the money you remember:

- large white £5 notes;
- £1 notes;
- ten shilling notes;
- crowns;
- half-a-crown;
- florins, two bob;
- one shilling;
- sixpence, a tanner;
- threepenny bits – (silver 'Joeys' or 12-sided copper ones);
- pennies, halfpennies and farthings.

There were:

- 2 farthings to a halfpenny;
- 2 halfpennies to a penny;
- 12 pennies to a shilling;
- 20 shillings to a pound;
- 240 pennies to a pound;
- 960 farthings to a pound!

Compared with decimal coinage, a penny was large and heavy, so if you were lucky enough to have a pocketful of copper, you knew about it. It might also be worth pointing out that whilst counting in '£ s d' was not easy, you soon got used to it and rarely made a mistake – you couldn't afford to!

Reference points are always helpful, like what your father earned, how much pocket money you received (if any), or what could be bought for a specific sum, like half-a-crown or ten bob. For younger readers to make sense of this you can include the converted price in new pence alongside, as in Table 1.

Table 1 Pre-decimal coins and notes and their decimal equivalents.

Imperial	Decimalisation
1d	0.416p
3d	1¼p
Sixpence	2½p
One shilling	5p
Two shillings	10p
Half-a-crown	12½p
Five shillings	25p
Ten Shillings	50p
£1 0s 0d	£1.00

Street traders

If some of the following strike a chord, it is likely that a few anecdotes will also be forthcoming:

- the milkman, possibly with a horse-drawn cart, dispensing milk from measuring jugs ... and your Mum skimming off the cream;
- the coalman, and having to count the number of sacks to ensure you were not diddled;
- delivery boys on bikes with the large basket on the front;
- lamplighters with a long stick;
- the rag-and-bone man willing to consider anything (jars, old clothes, scrap iron, etc.) in return for a goldfish, a balloon or a day-old chick;
- the tallyman calling on a Friday evening (payday), often with more tempting bargains to keep the bill topped up;
- the Carter Patterson man calling if you left the 'CP' card in

the window indicating you required their nationwide delivery service;

- the muffin man with his deliciously tempting wares;
- the chimney sweep with his brushes and various paraphernalia;
- the pigswill man collecting any food waste;
- Gypsies selling anything from clothes pegs to ponies or offering knife-sharpening and fortune-telling services;
- the organ-grinder with his mischievous monkey;
- the insurance man calling for his money, or, worse still, the rent man!

Even the postman may have worn other hats, like delivering groceries to the more far-flung areas.

Dustbin collection

Those in the country may not even have been provided with this service, but then there was probably very little that needed collecting when so much was recycled:

- combustible materials went on the fire;
- potato peelings were used to bank up the fire overnight;
- other food waste went to the chickens or pigs;
- any unused vegetation went with the grass-cuttings on the compost heap;
- clinkers from the fire were re-used, with the remainder being kept to grit paths in winter;
- clothes were patched until no longer wearable, then were cut up for rag rugs;
- glass bottles were returned for the deposit;
- jars and other odds-and-ends were kept for the rag-and-bone man.

With no plastic or swathes of packaging, often all that was left were tin cans, which could be washed and used by children playing 'shops' and other games, or else buried in the garden.

Case study – Violet Kentsbeer

The muffin man used to come round ringing a bell. I never remember the tray of muffins on his head being covered, but it did not seem to matter, and anyway the air was fresh and clean. On Sunday, the fisherman came along with his white barrow, selling shrimps, winkles, cockles, etc., which came straight from Southend. They were a lovely treat for Sunday tea, especially with celery – winkles for Dad and shrimps between the rest of us, and we would get a pin and take the winkles out for Dad, removing the black bit first. Mum would soak them in vinegar – it cleaned them and gave them more flavour.

Our favourite was, of course, the sweet man; he came round with a small handcart painted white, bearing such a variety of sweets. There was always a crowd round him because the big decisions had to be made: with only a penny or ha'penny – sometimes only a farthing – we had to decide what we could get most of with our money. There were coconut strips in pink or white, covered in sugar – but they weighed heavy; liquorice tit-bits, and we looked anxiously to see if any coconut ones had been put in our bag; acid drops that nearly took the roof off our mouths; liquorice boot laces, and so many more.

Every now and again a man would come round with a small carousel on a cart. The poor horse – it must have been a heavy burden to carry around the streets, and in return for empty jam jars we would have a ride on the carousel. The ragman would also come round shouting at the top of his voice, 'Any old rags to sell.' If we were lucky, we got a couple of coppers or a goldfish swimming about in a little plastic bag of water. I do not know why, but the fish never seemed to live very long.

Points to ponder

- ✍ Excluding your family, who are the people you most associate with the area that you grew up in?
- ✍ What are your overriding memories of the neighbourhood?
- ✍ How has the neighbourhood changed over the years?

Top tips

- ✍ Write the way you speak – this way your character will shine through. If you are writing for a private audience, your readers are already on your side. They are not looking for a literary masterpiece, but a gentle read about you and your life.

- ✍ If possible, set aside an area in your home for writing. In addition to having everything already set up for when you feel inspired to write, you can store photographs, reference books and other memorabilia there to help with the project.

Childhood Days

4

Memories will continue to flow in this chapter as we look in detail at some of the many influences encountered during those formative childhood years.

Household routines

With labour-saving devices, efficient electrical appliances and such luxuries as fridges being largely a thing of the future, a great deal of effort was required in the running of a home. Even for those fortunate enough to have a daily, a live-in maid, or even a large staff to run the household, it is likely that much of the following will strike a chord.

Washday

For many, the Monday washday routine will be ingrained in the memory:

- filling the copper with buckets of water and lighting the fire underneath;
- grating bars of *Sunlight* soap, or maybe having the luxury of *Snoflakes*;
- using the 'dolly', 'posser' or 'ponch' in the tub;
- scrubbing the clothes on the washboard;
- rinsing the whites in *Reckitts' Blue* to make them whiter, possibly using water from the rainwater butt in the garden;
- the arm-aching turning of the mangle and the danger of trapped fingers.

You might like to describe the above process in detail as younger readers will have little idea about such museum-pieces as coppers, dollies, possers, ponches, washboards and mangles. Of course, you may have had one of the more sophisticated 'washing machines' with a manually rotated paddle.

There were no lightweight, non-iron materials, so heavy, water-laden cotton sheets took some hanging on the line, and it was not unknown for the line to break and the whole performance to have to start all over again! Great pride was taken in what was hung on the line – after all, it wouldn't do for the neighbours to see that standards were slipping!

If it was raining, everything would have to be hung on a clothes-horse or clothes-maiden in front of the fire, or on wooden racks suspended from the ceiling ... and then the air would be damp for the rest of the day. Perhaps a 'dry house' was provided where you lived; if so, explain how this worked and what happened if anything ever went missing.

Perhaps your washing was sent to the laundry, known in some areas as a 'bag wash'. With this service, the damp washing was returned later in the day, but it still had to be dried, ironed and starched.

External assistance was usually reserved for Dad's shirt collars, and if these were outside the household budget, it was a case of taking great care with the ironing.

Case study – Jean Dudley

Starching was an art in itself. First of all, the powdered *Robin* starch had to be made up; it was mixed into a smooth paste with cold water. Then came the tricky bit. Whilst stirring this mixture with one hand, boiling hot water had to be poured into the basin until the starch 'turned' – in other words, it became a thick clear jelly and was ready for diluting with cold water to suit the articles to be starched.

Ironing

Usually undertaken on Tuesdays, ironing was an art form all of its own, especially when using flat irons heated on the range. These heavy instruments provided good exercise, and quite a rhythm could be achieved by using two irons – one being heated whilst the other was in use. Electric irons helped considerably, and who needed stream irons when it was so easy to sprinkle water on clothes that were too dry!

Case study – Violet Kentsbeer

Washing really was hard work; I hated Mondays when Mum always did hers. First the clothes were soaked, then scrubbed on a wooden rubbing board – later the rubbing part was made of glass, which made things a little easier. The clothes were then boiled in a large stone copper heated by a fire underneath; the wood or coal was fed through a trap door in front of the boiler. After this the clothes were rinsed, first in cold water, then a second cold rinse with a blue bag to keep the whites whiter than white. The next step was to separate the articles to be starched: Dad's collars (these were separate from the shirt), pillowcases, etc. At last they went out in the yard (no garden) to dry. If it was raining, the clothes were dried on a pulley in the scullery.

When the clothes were dry, then came the ironing. There was no electric iron, of course – another invention of the future. Flat irons were placed on the top of the range, and to test whether the iron was hot enough one spat on it – if it sizzled, away you went on the table covered with an old blanket … there was no ironing board.

Cleaning

Cleaning was another of the major weekly undertakings as it was amazing how much dust and soot was generated from open fires … and how the fur balls collected under the beds was anybody's guess. Polishing and dusting were other regular tasks, along with cleaning the brass and silver.

Then there were the rugs and coconut mats forever ingrained with dust, no matter how vigorously they were thrashed on the washing line. The lino throughout the house would have to be washed, and any carpets swept, 'Ewbanked', or even 'Hoovered' by those who had such expensive luxuries, perhaps damp tea leaves being scattered first to help deal with the dust. The area between the carpet and the wall would also demand attention, including up the stairs.

Brasswork on the front door would be tackled with *Brasso*, and the step with a donkey stone – indeed, these duties may well have been undertaken daily, such was the concern over what the neighbours might think!

There was also the annual spring-clean, when even beds might be dismantled and cleaned before being reassembled. During this hectic activity, what would your mother, or her help be wearing – apron, gloves and even a scarf on the head?

Cooking and baking

This was usually left to nearer the end of the week, especially if Sunday tea was a special event or if visitors were expected. Perhaps you can recall some of your favourite recipes and helping Mum to taste the cake mixture!

Few people ever went on a diet … it was more a case of having enough to keep body and soul together in the first place. Pies, suet puddings and plenty of potatoes were great for bulking up on stodge, and there was invariably a pudding on the table: maybe a favourite like jam roly-poly, spotted dick, treacle pudding, etc.

With routines being a strong feature of everyday life, some people may even be able to remember what meal was associated with each day of the week. Monday was usually pretty standard: the leftover of the Sunday joint served up with bubble and squeak – ideal and easy to prepare in between the rigours of washday.

Other days of the week may well have seen casseroles, stews, liver and bacon, toad-in-the-hole, pies, faggots, fritters, dumplings, and, of course, fish on Friday. With every penny counting, perhaps you were served chitlings, sweetbreads, lights, braised heart, kidneys, tongue, brawn, brains and oxtail. You might like to record some local recipes or individual concoctions your mother favoured, or those developed by accident which have now passed into family folklore.

Case study – Mary Wallwork

One evening, when my grandfather was alone in the house and indulging his passion for reading, he decided to make himself a cup of coffee. He wandered into the pantry where he relied on knowing where everything was, as there was no light. He found the bottle of *Camp Coffee* and made his drink as usual with boiling water, milk and sugar. He then returned to his reading to discover he had made himself a cup of *HP Sauce*!

Chicken can now be eaten every day of the week, but in your childhood it is likely to have been a great rarity, possibly seen only at Christmas … unless there was an old boiler, which was still tough despite having been cooked for hours! Your Sunday joint might even have been roasted by the baker – a service costing sixpence or so.

It is unlikely that pasta, curry or any other foreign food featured on the menu, rice being reserved for rice pudding, along with other milk puddings like tapioca, sago and semolina.

Seasonal food

What fresh food you ate was dependent on what was in season, either from the garden or in the shops. If you grew your own and had a surplus, some might have been stored – potatoes and other root vegetables being interlaid with soil, and possibly straw, in 'clamps' or 'pies'. Other vegetables may have been pickled, and fruit made into countless pounds of jam – perhaps you remember picking the blackberries, gooseberries and raspberries?

Shopping

With no fridges or freezers, shopping was a regular event, and whilst few mums went out to work, those who did could find it difficult getting to the shops. Opening hours were usually 9.00 am to 5.00 pm six days a week, and for some it was a case of shopping on a Saturday afternoon and taking potluck as to what was left.

You may have had a good selection of shops on your doorstep, or perhaps used one or two local shops regularly and then travelled further afield for occasional items like shoes, clothes and material. Describe your experience, tying this in with the delivery system discussed in the previous chapter. If there was a local market, this will also need to be mentioned, especially if you went shopping just before it closed on Saturday to buy produce being sold off cheaply.

Mealtimes

With family life usually revolving around mealtimes, these occasions can provide some interesting insights:

- the pattern of meals on weekdays and where you ate;
- who sat where and any associated problems this caused – for example, if the person closest to the kitchen had to fetch and carry, and where the warmest and coldest places to sit were;
- how the meals were served, whether they were brought in on the plate or dished up at the table;
- whether grace was observed, who said it and what the words were;
- what foods you disliked and if you were allowed to pick and choose;
- what the repercussions were for not eating everything on your plate;
- the practice regarding seconds;
- whether you were allowed to speak at the dinner table, and, if so, what the usual topics of conversation were;
- how you excused yourself on leaving the table, perhaps having to ask permission;
- what happened if anyone was late for meals;
- how mealtimes differed at the weekend;

🖎 the ritual of Sunday lunch, and if Dad went to the local for a pint beforehand;

🖎 who did the washing up and how it was organised;

🖎 the routine for supper, if you had this;

🖎 what snacks, if any, you were allowed during the day;

🖎 what happened if the telephone rang during mealtimes, assuming you had one.

Don't forget to write about special meals like Christmas dinner, or any occasions when something out-of-the-ordinary happened at the dinner table, like some momentous news being broken. There may also be some stories relating to when friends or the wider family came to dinner.

Bath night

The weekly ritual of having a bath and washing your hair was quite an event, all the more so if it involved a tin bath in front of the fire. It might sound romantic to have a bath in front of a lovely warm fire, but the reality could be quite different, especially in large families on cold winter evenings. If this was your experience, describe the routine:

🖎 how the water was heated;

🖎 how it was transferred to the bath;

🖎 where the bath was positioned;

🖎 what the order of bathing was … and why;

🖎 how deep the water was;

🖎 what the water was like for the last in line;

🖎 what privacy was provided … if any;

🖎 what age this continued up until.

You might also like to mention the importance of ensuring that you got out of the bath on the side next to the fire, otherwise you would freeze to death!

Hair

For boys, hairstyles were usually quite easy – a crew cut or short-back-and-sides, but for girls it was a totally different procedure, whether it was long straight hair, plaits, or curls and ringlets.

Case study – June Brandon

After a while, Sylvia and I lost our curls, so Mum tied our hair in rags; the strips were plaited through the hair and twisted before tying. It was quite painful at times to sleep in them, but come morning our hair looked beautiful and curly (well, we thought so!), and we thought it was worth the effort.

As we got older we used tongs, which were heated on our black stove. Sometimes they singed our hair. Or we used 'dinky curlers' – a silver metal contraption that gave more of a wave than a curl. If the hair wasn't properly wrapped around the curler, the ends would stick out instead of curling. Dad's pipe cleaners came in handy as curlers too. I cannot recall ever having our hair washed with water from the tap – it was always rainwater taken from the water butt in the garden. Mum would rinse our hair with vinegar in the last rinse, to make it shine.

Then there were other problems associated with hair.

Case study – Mary Robinson

… there was an outbreak of hair lice – nits. Both Donald and I got them but George and Peter didn't. Every morning and evening Mum had to comb our hair with a special fine 'nit' comb. Donald's hair, being short, was no problem, but mine was a different kettle of fish. It was long, down past my waist, and I sat on a stool on the bathroom lino with a newspaper under it to catch the nits as they dropped out and were crushed.

Bedtime routines

Bedtime might have been chaotic as you fought with siblings, or you may recall a more tranquil regime. Either way, certain elements may spark a story or two:

- what you wore to bed;
- getting changed in front of the fire in the winter, and then racing up to the freezing-cold bedroom;
- getting younger siblings ready for bed, and the hassle involved;
- having a wash and going to the toilet … possibly at the end of the garden;
- cleaning your teeth, with salt, carbolic powder, dental cream, toothpaste or perhaps dentifrice;
- being read to by Mum, Dad or an older sibling, and some of your favourite books;
- listening to the wireless – perhaps you can remember favourite programmes and characters, and even theme tunes like the Ovaltineys;
- the type of hot water bottle you had in winter;
- saying your prayers;
- reading in bed, and the repercussions if caught!

Chores

As a child it is likely you would have had your share of household chores, possibly even receiving some pocket money in exchange. Perhaps these included:

- taking the wireless accumulator to be charged, and being careful not to spill any acid down yourself;
- black-leading the grate with *Zebo*;
- gathering rabbit food;
- polishing your shoes;
- making your bed;
- cutting up the newspaper into squares to be used in the toilet;

- feeding the hens, and possibly even gleaning the fields for corn;
- collecting the eggs;
- kneading dough – after all, the family consumed so much bread;
- collecting kindling;
- making up the fireplace;
- collecting water;
- emptying the guzzunder!

Other chores are sure to spring to mind … and what was the outcome if you failed to pull your weight?

Earning a few bob

Whether or not you received any pocket money, you may have found other ways of earning a few bob:

- collecting jam jars, old clothing or anything else for the rag-and-bone man;
- scrounging empty bottles to return to the shop;
- chopping wood;
- following horses to collect and sell the manure;
- running errands, and hopefully being given a few pennies of the change.

Case study – Ken Baxter

An initiative was introduced which was a nice little earner for us. Bourne Forestry Commission was keen to establish more oak trees in the area and asked local school children to collect acorns. During the autumn we were encouraged to collect as many as possible, and with the offer of 3d per stone, we needed no second invitation. Each Monday morning children would arrive at school pushing wheelbarrows with sacks of acorns. Marian and I would usually end up with a shilling or perhaps 1/6 to share ... but this soon disappeared at the sweet shop.

The more formal jobs you had during your school years can also be considered:

- helping with a milk round;
- having a newspaper round, or perhaps making deliveries for the grocer, butcher, baker, etc.;
- working on a farm;
- a weekend job working in a shop;
- running errands for a few regulars;
- gardening;
- hop-picking or helping with the harvest;
- helping with the funfair or circus.

You might also want to include bob-a-job weeks if you were in the Cubs or Scouts. Any imaginative and not altogether legal forms of making money will also be fascinating for your readers if you feel honest enough to include them!

Spending the money

It was always easier to spend any hard-earned money, and there was no shortage of choice.

Case study – Betty Grainger

With money in our pockets we would head towards town and the cinema, often stopping at the sweet shop, or maybe the chip shop, which sold bags of 'crackling' from the fish for just a penny. No thought was given to cholesterol or getting fat – it simply tasted divine. Alternatively, there were the 'knockings', the stale day-old buns. These were great value at a bag for a penny.

Once in the cinema we would escape from the real world with such heroes as Roy Rogers and his horse Trigger. Gaby Hayes and the Lone Ranger flashed across the screen while we gasped in awed admiration. Nails bitten to the quick, we sat on the edge of our seats waiting for the next instalment when a card was shown, '… to be continued next week.' We headed back home re-enacting the adventures of our heroes.

Leisure hours

You might like to describe how you spent your leisure hours, when not doing your chores or homework (if you were given any), and how this differed throughout the seasons. In the long winter evenings you are likely to have been cooped up in the same room as the rest of the family, as this was probably the only place with any degree of warmth.

The wireless

The wireless was the highlight of most evenings. You are sure to have had your own favourites, but perhaps some of those listed below were among them:

- Much Binding in the Marsh;
- The Man in Black with Valentine Dyall;

- ITMA with Tommy Handley;
- Around Town;
- Children's Favourites with Uncle Mac;
- Listen with Mother …'Are you sitting comfortably? Then I'll begin …';
- Mrs Dale's Diary;
- Educating Archie;
- Top of the Form;
- Take it From Here – with the Glums.

Other indoor activities

These may have included:

- writing letters or keeping a diary;
- knitting, crocheting, cross-stitch or dress-making;
- making rag rugs;
- filling in your scrapbook;
- doing jigsaws;
- practising your cat's cradle;
- writing and performing plays for family and friends;
- hobbies like collecting stamps or cigarette cards;
- playing cards and board games, darts and shove ha'penny;
- making pom-poms from the cardboard milk bottle tops;
- practising the piano and maybe even singing around it as a family.

Case study – Robert Measures

We used to cut around the lifebelt surrounding the sailor's head from *Players* cigarettes, and then remove the portion within the lifebelt that was the background. The cut-outs could then be strung together by looping the belt over the sailor's head to form an ever-lengthening streamer.

Books and comics

When it came to reading, you might remember some of your favourite books: *Black Beauty, Anne of Green Gables, Little Women, What Katy Did, Biggles, Jennings,* etc., and popular authors included Enid Blyton, G.A. Henty, A.A. Milne, Richmal Crompton, Noel Streatfeild and Rudyard Kipling.

As for comics, there was no shortage of choice: *The Hotspur, The Wizard, Girls' Crystal, The Beano, The Dandy,* etc., or perhaps you preferred the more cultured *Boy's Own* or *Girl's Own?* There were also newspaper comic strips – maybe your favourite was Rupert Bear, or perhaps Teddy Tail in the *Daily Mail?*

Outdoor activities

With few cars parked in the street and not many more being driven around, perhaps you played in the street … always assuming this was not frowned upon by your mother. Wherever you played, you were unlikely to get bored:

- skipping to various rhymes – 'All in together, girls …';
- hopscotch;
- marbles – 'glass alleys' or perhaps 'bollys' (large ball bearings);
- tincan Tommy;
- conkers … and all the devious methods of hardening them – soaking in vinegar, baking in the oven, etc.;
- football with jumpers as goalposts and the heavy leather, laced ball;
- cricket in the street with the stumps chalked on a wall;
- egg collecting and blowing;
- jacks or fives (onesy, twosy, threesy, foursy, fivesy, crab, cricket and lobster);
- riding your *Fairy* cycle;
- playing with a hoop and stick, top and whip, hoop-la or spinning top – not forgetting the coloured marks chalked on the top which looked great when it was spinning;

- bird watching;
- fishing or collecting tadpoles;
- climbing trees;
- kiss chase;
- autograph hunting – footballers and cricketers – possibly even actors if in a large city;
- swimming or water polo;
- going to the cinema and sneaking in through the fire escape or some other scam!

Group games included 'tag' or 'tig', 'The farmer wants a wife', 'In and out the woods of bluebells', 'British bulldogs' or 'What's the time, Mr Wolf?' There were also ball games – bouncing one or two balls either against the wall or on the ground. These had various degrees of difficulty: two hands, one hand, throwing the ball from under your leg, then on one leg and finally on your knees. As if this was not tricky enough, a rhyme also had to be sung, such as:

> Each peach pear plum, where is Tom Thumb?
> Tom Thumb is in the house, where is Mickey Mouse?
> Mickey Mouse is in the cellar, where is Cinderella?
> Cinderella's in the wood, where is Robin Hood?

Then there was 'Knock-down Ginger', also sometimes known as 'Knocking dollies out of bed' with its associated rhyme:

> A house to let,
> A house to pay,
> Knock at the door
> And run away.

The more adventurous might even have tied door-knockers together to catch several people at once. As few housewives went out to work (except during the war years), there were usually plenty of unsuspecting victims!

Getting into trouble

Perhaps the park keeper was forever blowing his whistle at you, or you had the occasional clip around the ear by the village Bobby trying to keep you in order, and what were the repercussions of scrumping? Then there was placing a ha'penny on the railway line … but not too often as it meant going without sweets! The more mischievous the activity, the more interesting, and poking fun at yourself provides licence to do the same to others.

Case study – June Brandon

There is a ford in the River Rib, and rough ground sloped down to the water, then up the opposite bank to the roadway. The thrill of riding our bike (yes, bike – one between us!) down the slope, into the water and hopefully up the other side, was good fun. Of course we never made it right up the other side, as it didn't matter how hard or fast you pedalled, the bike always stopped in the middle of the ford. More wet feet for Mum to be cross about! We used to hit the socks against the stone bridge in an attempt to dry them. As this was never satisfactory, we would end up hiding the wet socks behind the wooden mangle, hoping she wouldn't see them – but she always did!

Religion

It is worth including what part religion played in your early life, and any associated teaching, choir practice, parades or youth clubs. No involvement also warrants a mention, simply because this would have been unusual. You may have been involved in a faith different from the rest of the community, or have grown up overseas and experienced a totally different culture and tradition. If so, there is all the more reason to write about it.

Case study – Betty Grainger

Once in a while the Missionary Society put on special shows. Tony, Billy and I would turn up early to ensure a front seat. We brought mugs with us, and also a ha'penny each, which would ensure a mug of cocoa and a bun. Sitting munching and drinking, we would be transferred into another world.

Slides were shown using a machine called a lantern projector. We would gasp in awe as wild animals sprang to life. There would be slides of lions, tigers, wildebeest and elephants; pictures of people so black that we screamed in terror … we'd never seen a black person before. We saw pictures of huts made of mud bricks and they had a sort of grass roof. There were no toilets, and the water was collected from a well. Washing was in a river – were there no washhouses? Women carried babies on their backs – did not all babies have prams? White teachers were in classrooms in the open air, and the children sat on the ground. After the show, we would head home re-enacting different characters, be it human or animal.

Explaining where your parents stood as regards their faith and any local involvement is a good place to start. If they were active, it is likely that you would have followed suit … either willingly or grudgingly. Some parents were quite keen to encourage their children to go to Sunday school, even if they themselves did not go to the church, simply to buy themselves some free time.

You might like to describe what and who your early influences were and, if relevant, what led to any decision of commitment. It will be interesting for your readers to see how your faith grew or diminished over the years, particularly if you now hold different convictions from those your parents encouraged … their reaction could also be significant. If relevant, this section also provides an opportunity to formally acknowledge those who played a formative part in the development of your faith.

Case study – Bill Barton

I cannot write of friends without mentioning the Scottish Schoolboys' Club (SSC), which has had such an impact on my life. Originally called The Schoolboys' Missionary Camp, it was the vision of Stanley Nairne, who with a few close friends took boys camping in 1912; its success ensured an annual series of Scottish Schoolboys' Camps. Stanley was ably helped by so many, and whilst Sandy Sommerville may have been the most memorable, Alistair, or A.B. Wallace, had possibly the greatest influence through my formative years.

I met 'Abe', as he became known to me, in 1937 at my first Scottish Schoolboys' Club Camp at Naemoor when he was the Marquee Officer. Abe was a renowned plastic surgeon and general paediatric surgeon. I will never forget that experience, standing at the fire in front of Abe, his arm placed round my shoulder. As my group was called out he gripped my shoulder and gave me that wonderful feeling of friendship. It was a deep emotion for a young lad who had not seen his parents for three years. The experience made me realise I was not alone, but surrounded by a wealth of friends and a spirit of Christian fellowship. It was at these Scottish School Boys' camps that I was able to find the true meaning of the Christian faith for myself, and how I could be involved with that throughout the world for the rest of my life.

Societies and clubs

Involvement in organised activities should not be overlooked:

- Cubs and Scouts, Brownies and Guides – the badges you earned, the seniority you achieved and the camps you attended;
- Boys' and Girls' Brigade;
- Sea, Air or Army Cadets;
- The Woodcraft Folk;

    ℣ any organised team sports – football, cricket, rugby, netball, lacrosse, etc.

Special occasions

Christmas

How you celebrated Christmas as a child will probably be quite different from how it is celebrated today, thereby providing plenty of material for your book. Perhaps this included a neighbourhood Christmas party, or one arranged by your father's employer. There might also have been an annual pantomime. Other things to describe include:

    ℣ making and sending Christmas cards – not to everyone, though, only for those you hadn't seen during the year;

    ℣ your expectations leading up to the big day;

    ℣ preparations like plucking the chicken, picking sprouts, etc.;

    ℣ decorating the house – making paper-chains with flour and water paste, putting candles on the Christmas tree (if you had a tree) and hanging up the stockings;

    ℣ where you celebrated Christmas, not forgetting any relatives who came to stay;

    ℣ carol singing, the nativity play at school and a church service;

    ℣ leaving out the mince pies and milk … or did Dad prefer something stronger!;

    ℣ trying to stay awake to see Father Christmas;

    ℣ what you usually had in your stocking – nuts, orange …;

    ℣ when you opened your presents and the type of presents you received;

    ℣ any special presents you still remember with affection;

    ℣ family traditions, like playing charades, or cracking walnuts with a flat iron on top of the range or on the concrete floor.

Other special occasions

These might include:

- birthdays;
- New Year's Eve – particularly in Scotland;
- Easter;
- May Day;
- Harvest Festival;
- Empire Day (24th May);
- Guy Fawkes' Night.

The foods, customs and any special clothing associated with these and other festivals may be of interest, especially if you came from a different culture and had your own traditions.

There were also one-off celebrations like VE-Day, and the coronations of King George VI and Queen Elizabeth II. If any of these were in your childhood years, they should be considered in your writing. The history notes at the end of this book may be helpful here.

Holidays

Holidays in your childhood are worth recording, and if you never had a family holiday that should also be mentioned as it will be quite alien to current expectations. Even a day trip in a charabanc to the seaside with the Sunday school, or perhaps a working holiday like picking hops in Kent will provide plenty of material. You might like to consider:

- how much time off work your father received each year;
- where you went on any holiday/day trips;
- how you travelled there and any games you played on the way;
- whether the luggage was sent in advance – perhaps by *Carter Patterson*;
- who you went with;

- the accommodation and any memorable landladies;
- how people dressed on the beach – including yourself and your parents;
- the bathing attire, especially if it involved knitted bathing suits that filled with water;
- the food you ate;
- your favourite brands of ice cream: *Lyons, Eldorado*, or the 'Stop me and buy one' *Wall's* man on the tricycle selling *Snofrute* and *Snocreem*.

Case study – Joan Kaemmler

During the train journey, Mum, Edna and I were wondering what the sea would be like and would it frighten us! The steam train finally arrived at Margate, the sun was shining brightly and Dad carried the suitcases – he must have felt very hot dressed in a suit, collar and tie, as always. Dad asked for directions to the guesthouse, and on turning the corner we saw the sea. It was magnificent, blue and sparkling, the sands were golden and there was the sound of laughter. There were shrieks of delight coming from children paddling in the sea and others making sand castles.

As we looked along the front we saw ice creams and spun sugar for sale, and a man selling chestnuts. From the nearby pub we could hear the drinkers, their voices raised singing, 'Oh, I do like to be beside the seaside'. I gasped with delight at the picture, a memory that would stay with me always. Gone was the first fear of seeing the sea; it was now replaced with an impatience to paddle in it and make sandcastles.

The lady at the boarding house was very pleasant and had a good meal waiting for us. So we spent a carefree week, paddling and eating lots of ice cream. The week ended with us all looking very brown and healthy. When I was much older I found a postcard that my father had sent to his brother saying, 'The holiday is wonderful and the children are enjoying it so much' – how right he was.

Clothes

The range, quantity and design of your clothes was unlikely to have been as great as they are today. It was more likely to be two or three outfits of hand-me-downs – functional clothes like those worn by adults but in miniature. With the absence of central heating, double-glazing, well-insulated homes and modern fabrics, clothes were of a utilitarian nature, usually worn in several layers in an effort to keep out the cold.

Case study – Jean Dudley

The only heat in the house came from an open fire in the dining room, and only on high days and holidays in the drawing room. The best place for warmth was to sit in one of the leather armchairs either side of the fireplace, and even then only the front of you was warm. It was very often a trip to the Arctic to go to the bathroom or to bed, and of course we had to dress accordingly. We children wore vests, liberty bodices, warm, bloomer-style knickers, woollen stockings and jumpers, and warm skirts. We never wore trousers, and as for jeans, they were not to make an appearance in England for many a year.

Even the eldest child in the family was not necessarily exempt from hand-me-downs, and especially during the make-do-and-mend war years clothes would be lengthened and ingeniously altered. Coats would be made from blankets, skirts from blackout curtains (perhaps brightened up by some ribbon), and, for the really fortunate, the odd garment or two from silk parachutes. Clothes would only be discarded when they wore out, not because you were bored with them or they went out of fashion. And any clothes beyond repair ended up as dusters, floor cloths or rag rugs. Some of the following are likely to strike a chord:

- combinations;
- liberty bodices … with rubber buttons to survive the ordeal of the mangle;
- corsets;

- bloomers;
- suspenders and stockings – using a sixpence when the suspender button fell off, and the countless hours spent repairing ladders in the stockings;
- sock suspenders for men and, for those with clerical jobs, armbands on shirt sleeves to keep the cuffs raised;
- braces;
- long johns;
- night-dresses and striped pyjamas;
- waistcoats and detachable collars.

You might be able to describe some favourite outfits, or perhaps those you dreaded even before they got to you because an elder sibling told you how uncomfortable they were. If brave enough, you can record how often you wore your clothes between washes, even the underwear! Sunday best can also be described … and what happened if you got them dirty when playing?

Headwear

Hats were a part of everyday life and usually reflected a man's job or standing in society. Then there were the associated courtesies, like men removing their hats when entering a house or church. You may also remember your father doffing his hat when meeting a friend or paying respects to a passing funeral cortège. Quite apart from her hat when she went out, your mother may have worn a headscarf when cleaning the house … and did she or your grandmother ever wear a hairnet?

School uniform

Children might remember losing their school hats, caps or berets – either by accident or design – or being caught not wearing them outside school and the implications of this. Wearing the school tie was also sacrosanct. Then there were the gloves and mittens threaded through the arms of the coat to save them from being lost!

Boys had to wear shorts, whatever the weather, and shoes were protected with 'blakeys' or 'skegs' in an effort to extend their life. With only one pair of shoes this was necessary, particularly if the shoes were worn for playing football … against the advice of parents! Clogs were favoured in some parts of the country; with their iron runners, these were great for sliding on the roads and seeing who could make the best sparks.

Discipline

When thinking about how you were punished at home, a few choice anecdotes are likely to spring to mind. The difficulty may be in choosing the appropriate incidents to share.

Case study – Elspeth McKechnie

The house next door was huge, and one summer the entire garden was planted with red geraniums. I took an instant dislike to these flowers and the small boy who lived there, so, armed with a pair of scissors, I cut off all the flower heads! I was caught, reported to my mother, and spent the remainder of the day confined to my bedroom.

I would always try to take Mike (our sheepdog) with me if I was in trouble as this helped lessen the punishment. My parents soon cottoned on to this and sent Mike outside, but he would then sit on the path below my bedroom window and we would carry on a conversation. I never believed I was really naughty, just high-spirited!

Illnesses

Prior to the advent of the National Health Service in 1948, GPs charged for their services. Some people paid 6d or a shilling a week to build up a reserve for when it was essential to see the doctor, otherwise it was a case of receiving a hefty bill. Many kindly doctors often 'forgot' to send a bill to their less well-off patients, but people still thought twice before calling the doctor.

Even then, some of the treatments left a lot to be desired and any stories about cupping, leeches or any similar Victorian remedies are well worth recording. In a time before Penicillin, it was a case of depending on all-purpose sulphonamides like M&B 693 and 760. Many homemade remedies are sure to spring to mind.

Case study – June Brandon

Our childhood ailments were treated with brimstone and treacle, syrup of figs or perhaps camphorated oil, which was poured on a rag and taken to bed to help us breathe freely through the night. Bread and milk would soothe sore throats and onion gruel would help to ease a cold. Cod liver oil and malt was given by the spoon, as was *Virol* for helping us to grow up strong and healthy. A clove was placed in a hollow tooth for that piercing pain of toothache, and warm olive oil was dropped into the ear and a warm scarf tied around the head for earache. As I suffered so much from these last two ailments, I well remember the comfort to be had from these remedies.

You may also remember the preoccupation adults had with ensuring you were kept 'regular'. If your parents were forever forcing something down your throat, or applying some concoction or other to keep you from death's door, perhaps some of the following may be familiar:

- bile beans;
- senna pods;

- iron 'jelloids';
- syrup of figs;
- *Radio Malt*;
- *Sidlets Powder*;
- zinc and castor oil;
- goose grease applied liberally to your chest at the first sign of a cough;
- mothballs in a muslin bag round your neck to clear the sinuses;
- sasparella to clean the blood – especially popular in the spring;
- penny royal, especially for girls as they started to develop;
- arrowroot biscuits.

Hospitals

Any broken bones or injuries requiring stitches might have necessitated a visit to the hospital, but there were also potentially fatal illnesses around such as polio, whooping cough, TB, meningitis and scarlet fever. Even if the nature of the illness meant that visitors were allowed, it was not always easy to accommodate the rigid visiting hours, especially as most people were dependent on public transport. With few homes having a telephone, a reference number was often allocated to the more serious cases so that local newspapers could print the patient's progress, and emergency announcements sometimes interrupted a film being shown at the cinema.

Visiting children was sometimes discouraged in case it was too upsetting for them when their parents left; it was not unknown for children to be strapped in their beds to prevent them running after their parents. If you were hospitalised during your childhood, or perhaps had a sibling who was, you may want to record the experience and the austerity of the place, especially the control exercised by Matron.

Dentists

Visits to the dentist also had their share of horrors.

Case study – Olga Moorhouse

The school dentist checked all our teeth in the morning, with the afternoon being reserved for any treatment. I received the dreaded news that I had to have a tooth removed and the 'big' girl who had been assigned to organise us remarked with glee that I would need a hanky '… because there'll be lots of blood.' She called me out of afternoon lessons to escort me to the dentist's makeshift surgery, a storeroom by the library. This vampire was enjoying herself regaling me with stories involving pints of blood … my blood.

The surgery was Dickensian – gloomy, cold and scary, and all the instruments of torture were in full view. He was a tall, thin man with a hard face, and when I entered the room he told me to sit in THE CHAIR. After probing my mouth he injected my gum with some kind of anaesthetic, the sight of the vast needle nearly making me faint. He then told me to wait outside.

Once again I encountered Dracula who did her best to reassure me, 'You will have to wait for it to go really numb because he will have a struggle to pull the tooth out.' The rest was horror and fear; my face was paralysed, I couldn't swallow and the final insult was that I had to go back to class until home time. I still feel ill when I think about it and, unsurprisingly, I am still terrified by the prospect of visiting the dentist.

Pets

If pets played a part in your childhood, they should be included, especially those treated as one of the family. If you had dozens of pets, you might like to draw special attention to the more significant ones. And what were they fed – leftovers from the table, or perhaps the cat was lucky enough to have 'pieces' bought from the fishmonger or the cat's meat man? You can also include some of the more unwelcome guests here, like cockroaches, flies, spiders, etc.

Travel

For most children travel meant shank's pony, unless they were lucky enough to have a bike. Transport in your childhood is sure to stimulate a memory or two, and there's no reason why you shouldn't start right at the beginning:

- prams, perhaps of the *Silver Cross* variety, being shared with one, two or more siblings;
- bicycles with stabilisers;
- go-carts;
- horse and cart – or scrounging a lift from the milkman or other delivery men;
- buses – single-decker or travelling on top of the double-decker;
- charabancs – especially for holidays to the seaside;
- electric trams – with the overhead power supply and trailing metal runners on the roof that often became disconnected and had to be realigned;
- steam trains – which sound romantic but that often left smuts in your eyes;
- ferries and steamers, especially on holiday;
- cars – for the lucky few, and perhaps the thrill of sitting in the 'dickey seat'.

Case study – Ann Davies

Queenie, Brenda and I used to sit in bed and look out of the window on to the road. There were very few cars about – they were strictly for the more well-heeled. One of the few cars belonged to Doctor Kendall, and we used to play a game to see who could spot his car first when he came home in the evening. I still remember the registration number: ARX 10.

(… and Ann was only born in 1936.)

If your father owned a car, did you feel privileged or assume that this was normal? Alternatively, describe the excitement of your first ride in a car – it will make for incredulous reading by those used to families with two or three cars today.

Difficult times

Childhood can be painted as an idyllic picture, but your experience may have been far from that. It might have been a case of frequenting the pawnbroker, borrowing from friends, the ignominy of the means test and watching bailiffs take whatever they wanted, or moonlight flits to keep one step ahead of the landlord. There may also have been excesses of drink, physical violence or other horrors that made your childhood a nightmare.

Case study – Marie Keating

One summer's day, when I was five, Dad announced that he was taking us on a train to a nice place near the sea. I was the middle of three sisters and we all screamed with delight, as we had never been on a train before. When I asked where Mummy was, Dad hesitated as he said, 'Mummy's gone away for a few days.'

We alighted at Middlesborough, and after a long walk Dad led us through a gate into some beautiful gardens. We passed a large attractive house as we skipped and danced our way down the paths between the lawns and borders festooned with colourful flowers. We chattered excitedly between ourselves wondering when we would see the sea, following Dad as he silently guided us on the way.

We came to a huge green wooden door, an iron bolt was slid back and Dad led us through. We gasped at the change of scenery on the other side; an imposing red brick building faced us, surrounded by a concrete courtyard, and to complete the glum picture huge walls cut off all outside views.

The door to the building was open and three black figures shrank back as if hiding from us. Dad kept guiding us nearer the open door, and looking through I could see a long wooden trestle table and bench. On the table were three white enamel plates with blue rims and mugs to match – on each plate was a wedge of bread and margarine. As we got nearer to the open door the black figures emerged and sprang into action, grabbing each of us. Our hearts told us something was wrong and we started to cry.

Amidst the ensuing screaming and scuffling I could see Dad slipping quietly away. Struggling with all my might to free myself from the grip of the strong arms holding me, I screamed, 'Daddy, Daddy, don't leave us!' I was terrified and tears streamed down my face as I heard my sisters also yelling in fear, begging him to come back. We watched in horror, realising all hope was gone, as Dad, his shoulders hunched, retraced his steps, not once looking back. He went through the green door and it closed firmly behind him.

What had been the start of a joyous day ended in horror and heart-break. Until now our existence had been with Mummy and Daddy each and every day. Instinctively I knew we had been abandoned. I can say no more.

When writing about difficult areas, care needs to be exercised, particularly if some family members may be offended.

Points to ponder

Assuming you didn't live in one of these places, describe the excitement of:

- your first visit to a large city;
- your first visit to London;
- your first visit to the country;
- your first visit to the seaside.

Top tips

- You don't have to include areas of your life about which you feel uncomfortable. You can skip over it, explain in the introduction that this is a selective autobiography, or write something like, '… the next couple of years were quite difficult, and are still too painful to write about now.'

- Use all your senses by introducing smells, textures, tastes and sounds into your writing. Photographs of your childhood may be in black and white, but there was nothing dull about that bright red polka-dot dress you wore for your seventh birthday. And if the sound of the cricket ball smashing through the kitchen window still haunts you, describe it.

Schooldays 5

This chapter will mean different things to different people. Some will wax lyrical about 'the best days of my life' whilst for others this section will warrant only two or three pages in their book.

Most will have completed their education at one or two schools, others will have hopped all over the place due to the nature of their parents' work, or perhaps because of wartime evacuation, a topic covered in greater detail in Chapter 7, The War Years – Part I. Schooling may have been disrupted by illness, some will have been educated abroad, others will have been to boarding school or even taught at home by a parent or governess. Whatever your experience, there will be plenty to record, not least because of the enormous differences when compared with today's education system. The ideas in this chapter can be used for each of the schools you attended.

First day at school

If your first day at school is etched in your memory, this will be an ideal introduction to the chapter. You might like to include:

- what you knew about school in advance;
- if you had any siblings already at the school and if so what they had led you to believe ... not always borne out by experience;
- whether you felt nervous, scared or excited;
- if your parents made anything special of your first day at school;
- what type of uniform you wore – if any;
- how you travelled to school, and who took you;
- whether you cried when you were left there ... or perhaps ran back home;
- your first impressions of the school and the classroom;
- the number of pupils in the class;
- whether it was single-sex or mixed;
- the class name – The Infants', Miss Moody's, 1A etc.;
- the name of your first teacher, including a description and any interesting characteristics.

Case study – Iris Fulker

My first day at school in 1936 was a bit traumatic. I desperately wanted to go and could not understand why my sister Peggy kept trying to run away. I went in the main entrance with Mum and as we passed the Headmistress's door, there was Peggy draped over a desk having her bottom smacked with a ruler. I cried for her, and my teacher Miss Almond cuddled me better. She smelt beautiful and was so kind and gentle.

School buildings

Just as you did when writing about your childhood home, close your eyes and mentally wander around your school. Start with the first classroom you remember and try to picture the room – where the desks/tables/benches were positioned, where the teacher stood/ sat, picture the blackboard, the boiler or fireplace, the clock, etc. How high was the ceiling, what colour were the walls, was there a sandpit, or even some sleeping mats for the youngest children? Perhaps you can remember some of the charts or displays on the wall – a map of the world (with the British Empire coloured in red), arithmetic tables, and the alphabet. And where was the cane kept? Where were the toilets, the cloakrooms, the playground, the Head's office? Perhaps there were some dividing doors to amalgamate two or more classes, and what about any distinctive smells associated with the classrooms?

Wider research

No research is usually necessary, but options are available. For example, if the school is still in existence, consider visiting it and maybe arrange to have a look around. If it has been converted into a private house, the occupants might be happy to show you around, especially as you will be able to tell them how the building has changed. If this is not possible, take a picture from the outside to show what the building looked like, perhaps either editing the picture or explaining that the conservatory and satellite dish were not there in the 1940s!

If the school has been demolished, maybe the local library or perhaps a museum will have some records about it. Alternatively, a book may have been written, either an official one or perhaps memoirs of a past student – a local bookshop or newspaper office might also be able to help.

Teachers

Teachers can be amongst the most influential people in our lives, especially as they feature at such a formative time of our development. Memories of the distinctive ones, for good or for bad, and their nicknames, are likely to be associated with an anecdote. Inspirational teachers, those you looked up to, or perhaps who saw something special in you, deserve special mention.

Case study – Vanessa Long

In some ways, I feel I ought to dedicate this book to my English teacher, Mr O'Regan. He was a short, thick-set, rather colourless man, but he was so encouraging to me. I recognised that he had faith in me, and that meant so much. Advice that he gave often came to me in later years and I always felt that if I had any aptitude at all, he did the best with it. I had hoped to meet him again at the School Reunion – some 41 years after I left. He still lived in Marlborough, but was not too well and could not attend. I wrote to him saying how fondly I remembered him and how grateful I was for all the encouragement he gave me. He replied and seemed to remember who I was … but how many pupils had he taught before and after me? I heard he died a couple of years later – dear Mr O'Regan.

Friends

School friends must not be forgotten – some may have become lifelong friends, or maybe even your spouse! Of course, there may also have been those you did not like … nor they you. Consider such things as:

- first impressions, and how these were subsequently reinforced or dispelled;
- nicknames;
- characteristics;
- notable features, colour of hair, etc.;
- who your best friends were, especially if these changed over time;
- rivals in the classroom or on the sports fields;
- troubles shared;
- games played;
- your secret aspirations ... and whether or not they were realised;
- those you admired ... and why;
- those you disliked ... and why;
- the bullies ... not forgetting to include whether you were a bully yourself!

The school day

The routines of the school day can provide interesting reading. You might include:

- the morning rituals before you went to school – getting up late, making sandwiches, doing homework, waiting for your little sister;
- how far it was to school, how you travelled there, and how this changed as you got older, for example cycling or using public transport;
- who you travelled to school with;
- whether you were given milk (usually warm having been next to the heater!) during the day – and if so what you used the cardboard tops for;
- what you did during your lunch-break;
- having to stand when a teacher entered the room;

- how you addressed teachers, to their faces and behind their backs!;
- what the teachers wore;
- what materials you used for writing – chalk, pencil, ink pen and the associated blotches all over your hands and clothes;
- how the school day ended – prayers, putting chairs on the table, etc.;
- the routine at home after school – a snack and a drink waiting for you, chatting about your day with Mum, or maybe going straight outside to play;
- the routine if you were a latch-key kid;
- what happened if you were late home from school – if someone went looking for you what were the repercussions of this?

The curriculum

Whether you were taught the 'three Rs' or something more sophisticated, you will undoubtedly have had favourite subjects, and those for which you felt less enthusiasm ... anyone who experienced the delights of Latin is likely to have an opinion about it.

Case study – Peter Deeth

Latin was a black spot for me, and Harry Harden, a strong disciplinarian, terrified us all. Before lessons began we were supposed to sit at our desks with the classroom door open waiting for the master to arrive. Often a lot of horseplay went on, but when it was Latin we were all meekly at our desks and you could hear a pin drop. Harry Harden had metal studs on his shoes and as he approached the classroom we could hear the 'click-click' of the shoes on the corridor floor. Terror!

Each boy in turn had to translate one sentence from the passage. Harry would start with some luckless boy at the front, and progress up that row of desks to the back, then across to the next row and so on, right around the class. As soon as he had started, we would of course all feverishly count the desks and try to make sense of our sentence before being required to open our mouths. Harry of course was up to this and would sometimes change to another part of the class and thus upset the apple-cart.

I was caught by this one morning and made a mess of translating my sentence. If you made a mistake you had to stand up and stay standing, feeling conspicuous and foolish. When your turn came round again, if you made another mistake, you had to stand on your seat, and if, heaven forbid, you made yet another mistake, you had to climb up and stand on top of your desk. I had had a very bad morning and was standing on my desk feeling very stupid when Harry made a pronouncement which I never forgot: 'If every mistake that Deeth has made was a pint of water, we would have enough to sink a battleship.' Titters all round, but not good for the Deeth morale.

The way the subjects were taught can also be considered. Was it by rote, discussion, dictation, explanation or private study? Did you use slide-rules and logarithm tables? Was homework set ... and if so, when did you do it? Were you tested, and if so, how? Did you have to walk to different classrooms, and which teachers were associated with which subjects? You might even be able to remember some of the quotations you had to learn by heart! Write about some of the more memorable subjects and those long since removed from the curriculum.

Crafts

Case study – Violet Kentsbeer

We were shown how to knit at school when I was about eight – wooden knitting needles and cotton yarn to start with. It was just plain knitting, making a dishcloth, but quite difficult for little fingers as the yarn kept sticking to the wooden needles. When we went up to the next class we were promoted to making socks on four steel needles. Talk about being thrown in at the deep end! I was all right until it came to turning the heel. What a lovely dirty pink mess I made of that sock, but I was rescued from finishing it by Mum and Dad deciding to move house.

Laundry

Due to the complex nature of washing, starching and ironing clothes, many girls were taught laundry in school, sometimes as part of more comprehensive housewifery or mothercraft lessons. These are worth recording for social history alone.

Cookery

If cookery lessons were part of your school experience it is unlikely that you will have forgotten about them … either the nightmare or the sensation just waiting to be included in your book. You might also like to record how your culinary delights were appreciated by your family.

Gardening

Many schools had a garden or an allotment, particularly during the war years. This may have opened up a hobby, or even a career, which extended into later life; alternatively it may have put you off the soil altogether – either way it is probably worthy of mention.

Case study – Barbara Cox

Alan was a small, quiet boy who sang in the church choir and spent a great deal of time working on his grandfather's allotment. This paid dividends because Alan went on to become a gardener and he did quite well for himself … his surname is Titchmarsh!

Other activities

Sport

If sport played a significant part in your school life, it should be included. Sometimes the most minor successes are worthy of record, especially if they would be a surprise to readers several decades later.

If your school had a house system for sport, what house were you in and what were the implications of this? What teams did you play for, and to what degrees of success or otherwise? Perhaps you hated such sports because of the way the teams were picked, especially if you were always last to be chosen.

The less popular sports also warrant attention, for example lacrosse or handball, and some schools had their own special versions of more traditional games. Then there was the torture of cross-country running, and the various dodges attempted to avoid it. Anything unusual generally merits mention, as do any injuries inflicted – either to you or by you.

Case study – Dr Elspeth McKechnie

During my first year at school I was somewhat rough in a game of netball and tripped up a fellow player. I was ordered off to attend to the small girl's injury. I tried arguing with the Games Mistress, but to no avail and so off we went. I found a First Aid box containing a bottle of iodine, cotton wool and bandages, and I remember the discussion which then took place. 'I don't want iodine on my knee – I'll scream if you put it on.' I had been reading a rather exciting adventure book, so I informed my patient that if that was what she intended to do, I would gag her, tie a tight bandage round her mouth, lock the door and throw away the key. High drama at an early age, but my words had the desired effect. Her face soon showed me that I was in control of the situation. I applied the iodine and bandage and am pleased to say that my treatment was successful. I assumed I was not reported to her teacher, or indeed her parents. I had treated my first patient!

Describing the PT kit might also be worth a sentence or two, and what were the repercussions if you forgot to take it to school – if you had to wear your underwear for PT, it probably didn't matter anyway! Also, if there were communal showers after games lessons, were these welcomed or dreaded?

Any stories with a wider historical appeal should obviously be included.

Case study – Hugh Maw

The father of one of my friends was a director of the *Dunlop* sports factory, which made Don Bradman's cricket bats. On one great occasion they brought him to The Downs to watch a cricket match in which I was playing. It was a memorable day but, to my sadness, Bradman had to leave early. Anyway, I scored a half century and, unbeknown to me, there was a reward for the highest scorer – a cricket bat signed by the great man himself, and I was the recipient. I was, of course, ecstatic and very flattered by all the applause and attention. I felt I had made the big time and dreamt of playing for England one day … sadly, it was never to be.

Music

Perhaps music was already a feature of your home life before you started school, but for some, music lessons may have been an introduction to a whole new world. If you were unaware of the pleasures that lay before you as you played those first few faltering notes on the recorder, try to convey this to the reader. Your school may even have had a choir or orchestra with which you were involved.

School plays

Any school productions are likely to have left a lasting impression and will undoubtedly spark the odd memory. If you had to appear in front of an audience, try to describe your feelings about it – trepidation, excitement, etc. You may even have kept some programmes or reviews that can be included in your book.

School clubs

Involvement in lunchtime or after-school clubs (assuming there were any) will be worth mentioning. There might have been a chess or nature club, Guides, Scouts, Girls' or Boys' Brigade, or even a cadet troop, particularly as war clouds loomed.

Religion

With formal religion being an integral part of the education system, it is likely to have played some part in your school experience. If you attended a church school, explain the implications of this:

- what part did clergy play in the running of the school?;
- describe a typical or memorable assembly;
- if there was a school song, when was it sung? You might like to include the song if you still remember it;
- if hymns were sung, which ones did you love or loathe?;
- if prayers were said during the day, when was this – first thing in the morning, at lunch, at the end of the day?;
- how did your faith grow or diminish during these years?

Positions of responsibility

You can record the pride you felt at being bestowed with your first position of responsibility – even if it was only ink monitor or milk monitor. Head Girl or Head Boy, Prefect, House Captain, or Captain of a school team all warrant attention, especially any stories related with them.

Case study – Elspeth McKechnie

One day, during my last year at school, I was on corridor duty. It was a very long corridor and one was not allowed to run down it. I boomed at a crowd of first formers, who were racing along, 'DON'T RUN – WALK.' There was a tap on my shoulder and I heard the gentle voice of my charming Headmistress saying, 'Elspeth – you'd be a marvellous Sergeant Major in the Army.'

(Elspeth became an Air Commodore in the RAF, so perhaps her Headmistress was not too wide of the mark!)

Achievements

Write about how success was rewarded at school – perhaps a gold star, or being allowed to perform tasks for the teacher, like handing out books. If there was a house system, points might have been awarded ... or deducted of course! Describe any prizes you were awarded and what for. If it was a book you still possess, what was the inscription?

Punishments

Forms of punishment and the way they were administered make for good reading, whether the punishment was justified or not – maybe it was for being left-handed! Perhaps the masters threw chalk (or something more robust like the blackboard rubber), twisted ears or pulled the hair at the back of the neck; or was it was a case of being given numerous lines to write, having to stand on the desk or outside the classroom, or being sent to the Head? Then there were the weapons favoured for corporal punishment, like plimsolls, rulers and canes.

Case study – Ken Baxter

'Raker' Day would gather all the boys in the school into the dining hall and line them around the walls. A chair would be placed at the end of the hall and he would shout, 'Bend over the chair, boy,' to the unfortunate victim. If you were a first-timer you might expect a quick swipe. But no, he would walk down to the other end of the hall, and as you were bent over the chair you would hear the running footsteps getting closer. The closer they got the more you braced yourself, until you could hear that he was level with you, then 'crack'. That would really sting. The momentum took him three steps past you before he could stop. He would then walk to the other end of the dining room and start the whole procedure again. I remember seeing him hit one boy clean off the chair.

The main topic of conversation one morning was a double caning that was to take place in the afternoon. The only two who weren't talking about it were Terry Green and me ….

It is worth including the misdemeanour, and whether there were any repercussions at home if your parents found out.

Highlights of the school year

Special occasions in the school calendar merit some description:

- May Day;
- Empire Day (24th May);
- Sports' Day;
- Founder's Day;
- Speech Day;
- Parents' Day;
- Christmas;
- Easter.

If you were at school at the time, describe how the end of the Second World War was marked. Any school trips or holidays also deserve attention.

Boarding school

Whether it was loved or loathed, boarding school usually provides plenty to write about. As the school became a second home, sleeping arrangements and the longer working day can be described. Also, due to the intensity of the environment, teachers and friends will have made a great impact on daily life.

Case study – Vanessa Long

I loved sharing a dormitory with five other girls. I had always been a giggler, but somehow at Marlborough Grammar this developed phenomenally, until practically everything was funny. However, uncontrollable giggles were a distinct drawback at times and we must have been quite a trial to Matron. She once had a friend and me doing lines when we could have been out playing tennis. 'Insolence and lying are despicable' – I don't know what prompted that, but I have never forgotten that sentence.

On another occasion, the prefects in Wye House had all gone to a concert. We decided to take all the sheets off their beds, knot them together and try to drape them across the front of Wye House – goodness knows why! We were caught and rather put out that Matron was 'mad at us' and was 'a bad sport'!

At the beginning of Lent one year we resolved to leap out of bed the minute the 'waking-up' bell was rung. I think it lasted about a week and was then conveniently forgotten after returning from a weekend at home.

Overseas education

Anyone educated abroad will also need to explain the differences in culture, climate, expectations, traditions and examination system. Children sent to Britain for their schooling may not have seen their parents for years, especially if the war intervened. Their guardians in Britain will need to be described in much the same way as parents, as covered in Chapter 1 – Meeting the Family.

Case study – Bill Barton

Miss Whyte, our landlady, was in her early sixties and, being a spinster, my parents did not consider that she would be either prepared or suitable to take on the responsibility of looking after two children aged, at the time, ten and eight. So Mum continued to look for an alternative suitable solution. One day Miss Whyte asked Mum why she kept on looking for a guardian – could she not take us on? It seemed that Miss Whyte had become very attached to the 'wee ones', especially 'the laddie'. So it was agreed that Mum would leave us with 'Auntie', and she set off in early autumn to rejoin Dad in Kenya.

How lucky we were to be left with Auntie, who was the most loving and adorable person. She certainly adored me, a feeling I can genuinely say I reciprocated. She did not spoil me but gave me every comfort that a child could ever have looked for. She never tried to usurp or replace my parents' affection or love for me, but constantly talked about them and kept them as the model for me to follow as the precious beings in my life. They were always to be considered, always to be remembered and thought about, never to be taken for granted, but rather always to be loved and cherished.

Alternative schooling

Those whose parents taught or helped at the school in any capacity will have their own special stories. Was favouritism shown … or quite the reverse? If it was embarrassing having a parent around all the time, give some examples.

Illness may have necessitated being taught in hospital, as in the case of Jean Durrett who had TB and had to lie on a specially constructed frame.

Case study – Jean Durrett

We learned simple arithmetic – sums to us – reading and writing. The writing was done in copying books and, while I was on the frame, the only way I could cope with books was to have them clipped on to a board which I held above me with one hand while I wrote with the other. We only used pencils, and, in time, I managed to write quite well.

Shortly after starting my schooling it was discovered that the TB had spread to my other hip and my spine, so I was taken off the frame. I was then turned over on to my stomach and placed in a plaster of Paris boat in order to keep my body stationary. I propped myself up on my elbows and enjoyed being able to look around. It was easier doing my lessons lying on my stomach as I could look down on my books and I was in a better position to see the teacher.

Illness may also have required home teaching, although some parents may have chosen this form of education for their children. If you were taught by governesses, personal tutors or parents, it will be interesting to explore the tensions between your home and school life.

Further topics for consideration

Accidents

Anything out of the ordinary can provide material for your writing: being sick in class, getting caught short, accidents or illness at school, a fire alarm … or even the real thing.

Crazes

Try to recall some of the crazes at your school. These might include:

- collecting cigarette cards – name the various series;
- marbles – describe any favourites;
- conkers – what was your highest scoring conker?;
- hoop-la – what was your best score?;
- playing with yo-yos – until they were confiscated;
- diabolo – and seeing how high you could throw it.

Sex education

The likelihood of any formal sex education was slim, and parents rarely talked about such matters. Indeed, it was not unknown for children to come home to find a new baby brother or sister … and they had not even been aware their mother was pregnant!

Case study – Olga Moorhouse

Sex education was what the girls talked about in the schoolyard.

Question one: 'Where do babies come from?'
Answer: 'Out of your belly button!'
Question two: 'How do they get there?'
Answer: 'If you kiss a boy, you get pregnant!'

When a girl reached the age of twelve or thirteen, she was taken on one side and told that she could soon 'start being poorly'. Auntie Maggie told me this because Mum found it difficult to talk to us about such things. The schoolyard buzzed with questions, 'Have you started being "poorly"?' Some of the older girls revelled in revealing the horrors of it ... the pain ... the discomfort ... the restrictions!

When eventually your time came and you thought that being this 'poorly' would carry you off, you were told, 'You mustn't go out with boys!' I loved boys, they played all the sports games I liked, and our Bill was a boy and I went out with him a lot. It was all very confusing! The next horror to be disclosed was, 'You must not have a bath or wash your hair during this time, or it could stop and this would be serious.' How I wished I had been born a boy!

Parental involvement in your education

You might like to consider how big a part your parents played in your education – something that may be easier to evaluate if you have since been a parent yourself. For example, did they listen to you reading and help you with any difficult sums ... or did you not want them to? Indeed, they may have been too pushy or perhaps constantly compared you with a more conscientious or brighter sibling. If so, how did you feel about this?

If parents' evenings were provided, did yours attend, and what did you think about such occasions – you may have been apprehensive, or perhaps forgot to hand the note to your parents in the first place! Of course, your parents may have been called to see the Head for some other reason. If so, it will undoubtedly be worth recording.

Examinations

Write about any important exams that were part of your school experience, even if they largely passed you by. Perhaps it was a very stressful time – not that stress would have been a word often used in your childhood! If you took Matriculation, perhaps you can recall the frustration of having to pass a certain number of subjects to avoid failing overall. In writing about exams, include such insights as nerves, your mind going blank ... or cheating!

What next?

Sharing thoughts and feelings is an intimate way of future generations really knowing us long after we have disappeared. Aspirations fall into this category, and this is your opportunity to record what you wanted to be when you grew up. Whether they were modest aspirations or wild flights of fancy, the reader will be able to assess how far, if at all, they were realised.

You might also feel comfortable in sharing how some of your ambitions were thwarted – the fact that you could not become a teacher because your parents could not afford the uniform to send you to grammar school, despite your passing the eleven-plus. Perhaps you were given an opportunity you did not pursue, or had to fight hard for a particular opening, deriving great satisfaction when you achieved your goal.

Whatever the aspirations, for most people it was a case of leaving school and getting a job. This will be considered in greater detail in the next chapter. However, for those who were able to pursue higher education, the remainder of this chapter will be relevant.

Further education and university

Especially if you lived away from home during your studies, this is likely to have been a very significant time in your life, developing your character and laying foundations for the future. As such, it is worth writing in some detail about these formative experiences.

If you returned to education after having worked for some years, this section can be addressed at the appropriate point in your story. Include such things as:

- first impressions of your new place of learning;
- your apprehension and excitement of what lay ahead;
- the course you studied and any memorable lectures or seminars;
- lecturers and tutors who left their mark for whatever reasons;
- friends made, and other students who were influential during this time;
- dealing with the opposite sex and any romances;
- societies and clubs you joined;
- how you spent your free time;
- your accommodation and its merits or otherwise;
- how you managed to fend for yourself, particularly if it was your first time away from home;
- how much you had to live on, how far this stretched and what you did if there was a shortfall;
- any jobs you had to help fund your education;
- the long holidays and how they were spent;
- the value of your experience, quite apart from what you learnt academically.

Case study – Barbara Cox

In October 1958, I left home to begin studying at The City of Worcester Teacher Training College, Henwick Grove, Worcester. My father took his holiday of one week and he and my mother went up to Leeds Central Station to see me off. While my mother was very cheerful, I was surprised to see that my father was crying and very emotional.

In those days, college was really an extension of school, with lots of rules. The coming of age was 21, and most of the women were 18 or 19, except for a few mature students who attended during the day. The men who had done their National Service were all about 21. On the first day, the male students were assembled in the hall and given a lecture by the principal about how the girls had come to college straight from school, and their responsibility towards us.

Our time was fully occupied with lectures every morning, followed by lunch and then more lectures until the early evening. We even had lectures on Saturday morning and no one was allowed to miss any. Except when out on teaching practice, most of our time was spent on the college campus. The doors were locked at 10.00 pm and if you wanted to stay out later you had to have permission. On Saturday evenings, we had a dance in the college hall, but this was only for students. We danced to records until the evening finished at 11.00 pm. There was a religious service on Friday mornings which was compulsory for everyone, both staff and students.

Of course, what you learned during this time was far more than what was on the syllabus.

Case study – Dr Bill Barton

Professor Dunlop always dressed immaculately with matching tie and top pocket-handkerchief. His advice to us was, 'Don't worry too much about the suit you are wearing; what's important in facing a patient is that you have polished shoes, clean collar and clean cuffs. When the patient enters the consulting room, get up, go to meet them and ask them to take a seat, sitting in front of them. Their eyes will drop – they will not look you straight in the eye. They will see your shoes, and from the state of them may form a first impression of your clinical standard. As you continue the consultation they will raise their eyes, but still not look you in the eye. Rather, they will look at your neck and see your collar – clean? Finally, when they are lying on the couch waiting for your examination, as soon as you place your hand on their chest or abdomen, their eyes will drop to watch your hand. What will they see? Your cuff. Those three – always remember: clean shoes, clean collar, clean cuffs!'

Useful materials to consult

For those who wish to undertake further research, the following ideas might be of use:

- search out any old school photographs, reports, prizes, books, etc.;
- if you are in touch with any old school friends, chat to them – you'll be amazed at the memories you stimulate between you;
- if your siblings went to the same school, repeat this exercise with them;
- if there are any school reunions, consider attending one;
- the website, www.friendsreunited.co.uk has led to countless people getting back in touch after many years, often also resulting in class or school reunions – you might like to arrange one!

Points to ponder

Decisions made at school, either personally or those made on your behalf, will have had far-reaching consequences. It can be an interesting exercise to review some of these decisions and contemplate their importance in later life. These might include:

- the schools you attended – if there was any choice;
- a teacher believing in you or inspiring you to follow a certain direction;
- taking a stand on a particular issue;
- not taking a stand and subsequently regretting it;
- standing up to a bully;
- passing the eleven-plus;
- passing the eleven-plus and not being allowed to accept your place;
- failing the eleven-plus or not being given the opportunity to take it;
- choices made in certain subjects;
- deciding to leave school;
- staying on at school – or not being given the opportunity to do so;
- not being able to pursue further education.

Also, what was your proudest achievement at school?

Top tips

- Draw on your emotions – outrage, fear, infatuation, embarrassment, etc. Even now, years later, we can cringe or feel embarrassed about some trivial event from our childhood, and schooldays in particular. Not only is this likely to make an excellent anecdote, you also have the opportunity to set the record straight and formally apologise.

    ❧   Be careful not to include too many dates. It is easier for your readers to know that you were nine years old than if you write 'in 1941' and expect them to remember that you were born in 1932 and then work it out. It might be obvious to you, but it is not necessarily so for others. Of course, from time to time you will need to include the year, and there's nothing wrong in occasionally combining the two bits of information: 'In 1950, when I was 18 ....'

Growing up and Early Work Experience 6

This chapter considers the formative years of your early working life. It includes growing up, early romances and learning about life, so even if higher education, the war or National Service coincided with these years, it is hoped that at least some of the topics will be relevant in the writing of your story.

Finding a job

When you left school you might not have had much choice about what job you took. Maybe some of the following case studies will strike a chord.

Going into service

Opportunities for going into domestic service may have been diminishing, but they were still the first choice for many.

Case study – Mabel Forsdicke

When we left school at 14, Mum registered our names with *Hunt's Domestic Agency* in London. She wanted us to go into the larger households so that we only did one particular job – whereas in a smaller house there would be a general maid to do everything. Beatrice, Mary and Ruth were all housemaids, but I was a kitchen maid.

I went to work for Mrs Garrett in a big house called Green Heys. There was a cook, a parlour maid, and a housemaid, and I was the between-maid, which meant that I helped wherever needed. The lady was very nice and motherly. She was blind, but that did not stop her from training us. I remember we had a huge hall with a marble floor with various items of furniture around. One morning the lady was lying flat on her tummy feeling under a chest. She called, 'Child, child, you haven't dusted under here.' We certainly learned to be thorough!

Starting at the bottom of the ladder

For those who could not wait to leave school, the world of work was not always as glamorous as they had hoped.

Case study – Joan Belk

My first job was in a fishing tackle shop, working in the back of the premises sorting out maggots. The van would deliver the maggots into a big empty bath and I would sort them out into smaller baths – big ones in the right, small ones in the left, and dead husks in the bin. Then I had to put them in clean bran so that they were ready – all of this for eight shillings (40p) per week … and I worked 52 hours!

My next job was cleaning in a bakery and grocery shop. Sometimes I had to dunk legs of ham and bacon, that hung from the ceiling in mutton cloth, into buckets of boiling water for a few seconds to drown the maggots on them – was I never going to get away from maggots! 'Joan, give your notice in and look for another job,' were my mother's favourite words.

Parental advice

You might have got a job at the place where your father worked, or perhaps a chance remark led to a career you never even knew existed whilst at school. However, often it was a case of parents knowing best.

Case study – Ron Larkin

I think the only advice Dad gave me was to choose what he would have called 'a safe and secure' job, one which you could progress through to better yourself in the future. He saw banking, teaching or the civil service offering such 'jobs for life'. Becoming a teacher would have meant going to university, or at least a teachers' training college, which I certainly did not want – nor did I have the patience that teachers need. I never really considered banking as an option, and to gain entry into the Civil Service you had to sit an entrance exam, which I could not even contemplate. A similar option was a career in local government, so with my exam results in my pocket I went off for an interview at the Westminster Guildhall, where I was offered the position of Administrative Assistant in the Department of the Clerk of Middlesex County Council.

For some it was a case of having to overcome parental opposition to follow the career of their choice.

Case study – Stella Wills

My mother was totally against my going into nursing – she had decided that it was only right that I should work with her in the café. However, I applied to St Mary's Hospital, where I was accepted as a cadet. Mum suspected what I had done and telephoned the matron to enquire if I was there. The answer she was given was that if a girl had chosen a nursing career against her mother's wishes then that was the sort of girl they wished to train.

Following the crowd

For many it was simply a case of taking what was available.

> ### *Case study – Ann Davies*
>
> When I left school I didn't know what I wanted to do, but I did know that I didn't want to work at *Crosbie's*, the local jam factory, and I didn't want to go to *Overton Paper Mills*; those were the two jobs where most girls went when leaving school. I wanted to be different ... but that wasn't to be. Needless to say, I was the same as the others and got the job I didn't want in the jam factory.
>
> (Ann also subsequently worked at the paper mill!)

Setting the scene

Whatever your experience, you might like to write about:

- how nervous you were on your first day;
- your first impressions on seeing your new workplace;
- the size of the establishment and how many other staff there were;
- how you travelled to and from work, or your accommodation if you 'lived in';
- what the work entailed and if you had to wear any special uniform;
- how much you were paid, and your hours of work;
- how much you gave to your mother and what you had left;
- what holidays you were entitled to and any shut-down periods;
- what the people were like – the employers and staff;

-   how you adapted to the work, and whether it was physically demanding, enjoyable, boring, etc.;
-   what you liked about the work … and what you loathed;
-   any special friends you made at work.

If you had several different jobs in your early working life, you can repeat this process.

Apprenticeships

Professional careers usually involved an apprenticeship, the contract often being signed by the father or guardian of the apprentice.

Case study – Douglas Badham

I started my articles with the accountancy firm of *Coats West Grimwood* in September 1932. Some firms paid a nominal wage to their articled clerks, others made no payment at all. *Coats West Grimwood* were in the latter category and, in addition, my father was required to pay a one-off fee of £250 to the partner to whom I was articled for five years.

Even in 1955 when Ken Baxter started his apprenticeship with *The International Tea Company's Stores*, to 'learn the art, trade and business of a Grocer and Provision Merchant', his father had to sign the indenture. This entitled Ken to the following weekly wages:

    ❧ between the age of 15 and 16 years: 55 shillings;
    ❧ between the age of 16 and 17 years: 60 shillings;
    ❧ between the age of 17 and 18 years: 65 shillings.

Joining the Services

Men who wanted to join a particular service often enlisted before being called up for National Service. Only a limited number of national servicemen could enter the RAF, and then not as pilots, and the Navy was open only to those signing on for a minimum of three years. Regulars also earned more money. Those who joined the services will find Chapters 8 and 9 useful.

Living away from home

If your work meant leaving home – probably for the first time – you will also want to consider:

    ❧ how you adjusted to living away from home;
    ❧ whether you were homesick;
    ❧ what the accommodation arrangements were;
    ❧ how often you were able to go home;
    ❧ what you did in your time off.

Those who lived in digs will have a rich fund of stories, not all of them good.

Case study – Ken Baxter

I booked in and the landlord showed me to my room. What a lousy dive, I thought. It was dark and dingy, and the furniture was so old that it must have come out of the ark. I looked down at the skirting board … a rat hole. Being brought up in the country, I knew a rat hole when I saw one. What's more, there was a little bit of freshly chewed wood by the side of the hole. I'm not frightened of rats, but there's no way I'm going to share my bed with one.

I lay on top of the bed fully clothed. I didn't unpack – in fact I didn't even open my suitcase. I didn't sleep all night – I may have catnapped, but I was conscious of every little sound.

Before work the following morning I had a look around town to see if there were any digs advertised in shop windows, but couldn't find any. I arrived at the *International* just before 8.30. The manager welcomed me and asked, 'Did you get fixed up with digs?'
'Yes,' I replied, '*The Lord Nelson.*'
'Where? *The Lord Nelson*? You're not stopping there. Go and get your case, we'll find other lodgings for you somewhere.' When I returned to the shop, I discovered, to my relief that the van driver had been sent out to find me some better accommodation.

Initiation rites

Young, keen and gullible new employees are usually susceptible for a 'wind-up' by old hands, including being sent for a long weight ('wait'), a left-handed screwdriver, a glass hammer, a bucket of steam or some elbow grease. If you were subjected to any such routines your readers will be delighted to learn of them. Similarly, it is worth recording rituals associated with completing an apprenticeship (getting your 'credentials') – in the print industry the newly qualified were immersed in a barrel of printing ink and all sorts of gunge.

Charles Durrett wasn't quite so gullible when he went to London for the first time to sign on for the Army.

Case study – Charles Durrett

At around 7.30 am, I found a barber's shop for a shave so that I looked reasonably respectable when presenting myself at the Recruiting Office. Having requested a shave, I sat in the chair and away we went. I noticed that the price of a shave was one shilling and sixpence, which I thought was a bit steep compared with back home in Gloucester. Having completed shaving me, and without my permission, I was treated to hot towels, facial massage and other pleasant attentions which were pushing the price up as I could see from the price list prominently displayed above the mirror. It occurred to me that the fellow had summed me up as a country bumpkin on his first visit to the big city. How right he was. Alas, it did not occur to him that country bumpkins are not necessarily as green as they are cabbage-looking.

When all the unasked for functions had been completed, I was fed a line that I had in-growing facial hair and that I needed a one and sixpenny bottle of special lotion to rectify this condition; this I declined. The total bill amounted to ten shillings and sixpence, which he appeared sure would be forthcoming. I asked him what my request was when I entered his shop and he replied, 'A shave, Sir.' I gave him one and sixpence, which was the price quoted on his list for the service, and pointed out that, as I had made no further requests, I was not indebted to him in any way. When he remonstrated over the balance, I politely pointed out that he must consider his loss the price of experience, which I hoped would dissuade him from trying to take advantage of the innocent in future. I have never since had a shave in a barber's shop.

Early work experiences

It is likely that you will be spoilt for choice when it comes to including stories about your early working life. Whilst you are unlikely to want to go into intricate detail about every facet of the job, there will be some anecdotes that will be too good to omit.

Case study – Ann Davies

There were several jobs that we all tried to avoid at the jam factory, the first of which was sorting apples from large barrels. They were preserved in a liquid acid that took my breath away; after working there all day I would end up with a chesty cough as it got right into my lungs. I hated that job.

Cleaning jam jars was another dreadful job. These would arrive by the lorry load and had to be washed and sorted into different sizes. They came on large wooden trays, and were dipped in a bath of warm water. Our job was to put our hands in the bath and wash the jars. Where they came from, I dread to think, but there was all sorts of filth in them – dirt, eggshells, cotton wool, etc. Many a time we would cut our hands on broken glass, but there was no health and safety, so we just had to get on with it. I would like to think that the jars were sterilised after we had them, but I never saw that being done.

There was also the old man who made the ginger beer in a large vat; his job was to stir it with a wooden paddle. This man forever seemed to have a cold as there was always a dew drop on the end of his nose … drip, drip, drip! Strangely enough, I have never drunk ginger beer since.

Earning money

At least going to work meant having some money in your pocket.

Case study – Sylvia Culverhouse

I left school soon after my 15th birthday at the end of the summer term in 1949. This was the first year that the school-leaving age had been raised to 15; up until this time children had left at 14.

Having passed an aptitude test, I was offered the position of clerk at the *Co-operative General Office*, at a weekly wage of 32s 6d. It was a 40-hour week, five and a half days, with one Saturday off in four. There was a week's holiday with pay, with half a day off to attend continuation college.

Out of the 32s 6d, I gave Mum 30 shillings and was allowed to keep the 2s 6d. As I was not used to handling money and going out and about on my own, I did not think this unfair. Mum and Dad had paid out regularly for my secretarial classes, and Mum had always made my clothes, so what did I want extra money for?

(However, Sylvia's contentedness did not last for long …)

It was in the February that I had my first rebellious argument with Mum. I was well aware by now of how the other girls in the office had much more spending money than me, and could go out and make their own choices about clothes and entertainment. I considered that 2/6 a week was not sufficient for my needs. Mum protested and said I wouldn't manage, but after a while she gave in and I was allowed an extra 10 shillings a week, but was then expected to buy my own clothes. I felt quite rich, and used to save one shilling a week in a Post Office Savings account for rainy days.

Social life

Having started work, and with at least some disposable income, it is likely that your social life will have improved. Consider such things as:

- your new friends, especially any notable characters and those you are still in touch with;
- scams you got up to, especially trying to beat any curfew;
- church groups and youth clubs;
- other organisations you joined, like a work's social club or a sports team;
- milk bars and coffee bars, perhaps with a juke box;
- watching various sports – football, speedway, dog-racing, etc.;
- dances you went to, and the ritual of finding a partner.

Cinema

Even if you have already written something about the cinema, describe how your tastes changed as you grew up. Who were your new idols and what were your favourite films? The cinema might also have become an excellent place for a date ... especially if you were unlikely to get much privacy at home. If you were there to watch the film, it often meant having to sit though the final part before seeing the beginning, but at least you could stay there for three or four showings ... as long as you stayed one step ahead of the usherette.

Fashion

Fashion probably had little relevance in your childhood, but you may remember looking avidly at magazine advertisements, or delighting in the glamorous film stars, particularly the American ones. Depending on when you were born, your own fashion attempts might have included:

- smoking to look grown-up – if so what brand did you favour?;
- experimenting with make-up ... including the reaction of your parents;
- having your ears pierced;
- wearing a hat;
- taking a greater pride in your appearance;
- learning new dances and looking forward to the next night out;
- having a 'grown-up' or fashionable hair style, perhaps a perm for the girls or a 'DA' and *Brylcreem* for the chaps;
- becoming a Teddy Boy, Beatnik, Mod, Rocker or whatever the current trend was;
- getting into 'pop music' – maybe skiffle, or Elvis Presley, Bill Haley or even The Beatles;
- perhaps you had your own *Dansette* record player and can remember some of your favourite records.

Case study – Vanessa Long

Toni home perms were starting to come on the market, and my mother and I used them quite often. It was a whole afternoon's job with innumerable curlers and lotions. Even then, our hair usually turned out frizzy and too tightly curled at first, but it settled down after a while.

Clothes were very limited and for my first 'date' all I had to wear was my best summer dress (nothing special bought for the occasion) and I worried and fretted that it might not be 'right'. There was no fashion market for teenagers (or 'teenagers' for that matter) at that time and everyone wore the same type of clothing appropriate to the event, irrespective of age. No make-up was worn by teenagers either, and I must have been at least 17 or 18 before I experimented with that.

The men could take fashion equally seriously.

Case study – Ron Larkin

Money was in short supply, but it was important that, even as a young lad, you found enough to have at least one suit, and that one had to be fashionable. Whilst we did not subscribe to the Teddy Boy fashion, there was a dress code almost bordering on the cult style which consisted of a 'sharp' suit – 'sharp' being the word to describe the accepted style in vogue at that time.

It consisted of a single-breasted jacket, usually with a one-piece back and a small single vent, no more than four inches in depth, and the lapels were fairly high-cut to facilitate the three or four buttons. The trousers, whilst not quite so narrow as drainpipes, would have turn-ups and the bottom of the leg measured no more than 18 inches wide. It was important that the shirt had a detached collar, which allowed us to wear cut-away stiff collars. These were always white and usually worn with white shirts, but sometimes they were teamed with shirts of a different solid colour or even stripes, being attached to the collar band at the back and front with metal studs. There was no better place to see a fine display of all this fashion than in the snooker hall above *Burton's* in Station Road, Harrow.

Smoking

If you smoked, when did you start and why? It would also be interesting to know what your parents thought about this, and if they were happy to encourage you. Then there are the various different brands. Which did you prefer and why?

- *Craven A* claimed not to affect your throat;
- *Senior Service*;
- *Woodbine* – known as coffin nails;

ও You were never alone with a *Strand*;

ও *Kensitas* which provided 'four for a friend';

ও *De Reszke* and *Passing Cloud*, preferred by the ladies;

ও *Churchill No. 1* were a bit more expensive – perhaps bought on pay day?

Romance

First dates, innocent crushes and awkward overtures to romance make for excellent reading.

Case study – June Brandon

The next morning I was given a uniform to wear, after which I was shown around the huge kitchen. Nothing had prepared me for the shock in store when at 10 o'clock sharp we went through to the counter of the NAAFI canteen and the shutters were lifted up. In front of me was a mass of blue uniforms … I had never seen so many men in my life! I felt so nervous and wanted the ground to swallow me up. I was so shy, and went scarlet. 'Hey, we've got a new girl,' someone shouted, and I felt all eyes on me. My hands trembled as I poured tea into the endless rows of thick white cups. It was the longest day of my life!

Another cause of embarrassment for me was the nickname soon bestowed upon me by these men. I was called 'bumpers' … for obvious reasons!

When writing about matters of the heart, include only what you feel comfortable about. There is no compulsion to use names, or you can indulge in some artistic licence and alter them, especially if you want to protect others. You might also like to write about unrequited love, again, without revealing names if that is your preference.

Even having been diplomatic in your writing, if you still feel uncomfortable about sharing your innermost thoughts, don't include them. Alternatively, if you fear that a spouse or loved one may take offence, consider asking them to read the manuscript. Your fears are likely to prove unfounded, but if action is needed the manuscript can be edited before any book is produced.

Ending a relationship

Whilst this was usually terribly traumatic, some people found easier ways round the problem.

Case study – Jean Dudley

I had just become interested in boys, but Mum often complained that I would never pass my school exams if I didn't study more. My boyfriend was called Philip, and we would take long walks together holding hands, with just a goodnight kiss … and even then this was at the end of my road. He would solemnly take out of his pocket a quarter pound of *Black Magic* chocolates which he gave to me. Philip never came into my house, and when I got tired of his company and didn't know how to tell him, my mother went to the corner of the road where he was waiting and broke the news to him.

Being home on time

Especially for girls, staying out late was always a bone of contention with Dad.

Case study – Barbara Cox

As I was still living at home, I had to abide by my father's rules, one of which was that I must travel home on the 9.50 pm bus and not the last bus at 10.30. Consequently, I always had to leave the cinema early – even though it meant that I never saw the end of the film! Years later when I was married and films were shown on TV, I saw the final scenes of all the films that I had missed.

One Saturday night I went to the cinema with Harold Snowdon, whom my father liked very much, but unfortunately we missed the bus ... the only time I ever missed it. Although I was 24, I was really worried about my father's reaction. A neighbour was waiting for the later bus and she told me not to worry. However, when we got off the bus at the bottom of Moor Lane, my father was waiting for me. He told Harold, who was 27, 'You ... home ... and never take my daughter out again!' Needless to say, he didn't.

Holidays

The first holiday without parents is always an exciting time. Perhaps it was abroad to visit a penfriend, or maybe to *Butlin's* with a group of friends from work – whatever it was, it is likely to have been a memorable occasion. You might like to consider:

- what your parents thought about you going away;
- who you went with;
- where you went and what the accommodation was like;
- if it was abroad, how you coped with the travel and any language difficulties;
- holiday romances;
- how it felt to be 'grown up';
- if you kept in touch with anyone you met on holiday.

Points to ponder

You might like to consider a few more 'firsts', although how much you choose to write is a purely personal matter. These may include:

- first becoming aware of the opposite sex;
- your first kiss;
- eating foreign food for the first time;
- your first alcoholic drink;
- buying a bottle of wine for the first time;
- your first trip abroad;
- your first journey in a plane.

Top tips

- By all means use a thesaurus to increase your vocabulary. However, if you then have to use a dictionary to discover the meaning of that word, don't use it in your book. It is clearly not in your everyday language and will sound false in your writing.

- It's more important to get the story down than to worry about spelling and grammar – it can always be tidied up later, if necessary.

The War Years – Part I:
Everyday Life in Britain 7

Your memories of the Second World War will depend on how old
you were at the time and in what capacity you were involved. For
some it was a time of great excitement and opportunity, others
witnessed horrific sights, experienced major upheavals and lost
loved ones. Whether you served in some capacity, or the war largely
passed you by, your life story will not be complete without recording your experience of these years.

Due to the breadth of material to be considered, two chapters are
provided. The first is for those growing up during the war years,
witnessing the upheaval and becoming accustomed to a different
way of life in Britain. The next chapter focuses on those who
served either in the Forces or in some essential capacity. Even if not
within your own experience, it is hoped that both chapters will be
of interest, not least for the first-hand accounts that are included.
You might also like to use the history notes in conjunction with
these chapters.

War clouds looming

Our view of the events leading up to the Second World War is naturally coloured by hindsight. We now know that Hitler was not going to be thwarted by the earnest intentions of Neville Chamberlain, but there were plenty of people who did not want to believe dissenting voices like that of Winston Churchill predicting a second world war within a generation. Objectivity will be difficult, but if you are aware of your thoughts at the time, they will make for fascinating reading.

Whilst you may have been too young or unaware of what was happening in mainland Europe in the late 1930s, you may have been conscious of the more obvious preparations for war, like the distribution of gas masks in 1938. It is unlikely that your parents discussed such issues in front of you, but there may have been tensions or telltale signs making you aware that all was not well. It is worth recording how the build-up to war affected your own life.

Case study – Leonard Hall

Things were moving on the national stage. German aggression in Europe was creating enormous international tensions, and war over German designs on the integrity of Czechoslovakia began to look more than a possibility. On 30 September 1938 the British Prime Minister, Neville Chamberlain, returned from a meeting with Chancellor Hitler; he descended from his aeroplane waving a piece of paper signed, as he said, by Herr Hitler and himself, and it was 'Peace in our time'. Rejoicing was great, and a cloud was lifted, but it was at the expense of a small Central European country and it was nothing to be proud of. It was not long before the serious threat of war re-emerged, and all Munich did was buy time. Descending from the international to the personal, it bought time for me. I have often wondered whether, if war had come in 1938, I would have found myself in the armed forces before I had established myself at *Clerical Medical*, and before I had taken any actuarial exams and then vanished into some entirely different career.

The outbreak of war

Even if the imminence of war went largely unnoticed, for anyone old enough to appreciate the significance, the date of Sunday 3 September will live with them forever.

Case study – Tony How

Soon after 11.00 am on Sunday 3 September, we gathered round our wireless to listen to the sad, weary voice of Prime Minister Neville Chamberlain announcing that a state of war now existed between Great Britain and Germany. We had already covered some of our downstairs windows with strips of sticky brown paper to minimise the danger of flying glass. We possessed a sturdy oak table and placed protecting objects round this to form a crude air-raid shelter. We had gas masks, which we had tried out – the 'elephant noses' gave rubber smells and breathing difficulties, and had been both annoying and slightly frightening. Then we heard the wailing of our first air-raid warning. My sister's friend Sylvia was at our house. Dad was convinced that he could smell gas, so we donned our masks. Then Dad decided to run home with Sylvia and nearly became the first British civilian casualty of the war – people with weak hearts should not run in gas masks! The 'all-clear' was soon given. A stray aircraft had been the cause of a false alarm.

Enemy aliens

On the outbreak of war, 'enemy aliens' (refugees and immigrants living in Britain) were vetted to ensure they were not harmful to the national interest. Tribunals were established and a classification system instituted. Those in category A were interned, category B were placed under certain restrictions, whilst those in category C were free to go about their business as usual.

Case study – Helmut Rothenberg

Before the tribunals were set up, internment of so-called enemy aliens took place on a completely random basis. Two policemen turned up and took one of my uncles away one morning, possibly because he had the wrong name … Adolf! Actually, to our great amazement, he was back home a week later. Uncle Adolf suffered from a lifelong constipation disease, a condition for which he took certain drugs. All he did in the internment camp was refrain from taking these special drugs!

In the meantime we became wise to the fact that the police were calling on houses early in the morning with a view to collecting male refugees for internment. My father, Uncle Justin and I made it our business to leave the house each morning before 6.00 for a walk on Hampstead Heath … where we met hundreds of other people like ourselves who apparently enjoyed taking the early morning air! The police came to the door every morning and, when asked to see the three of us, my mother told them that we were not at home. The two policemen smiled and told her that they would come back the following day a quarter of an hour earlier. This farce continued for about two weeks, after which the Government stopped the whole charade and Hampstead Heath became much less popular.

Being evacuated

Even before war was declared, the evacuation was well under way. In London alone, 4,000 special trains were laid on to transport 1.3 million official refugees. Many children went to live with relatives in safer parts of the country or abroad, and some companies arranged for employees' children to be evacuated to families in overseas branches.

If appropriate, try to include the intense feelings of fear, excitement, loneliness, camaraderie or whatever your experience was. You might like to consider:

    how you felt leaving your parents and/or friends behind;

    the excitement/apprehension of travelling into the unknown;

    first impressions of your new neighbourhood;

    the worry or even rejection of waiting to be chosen;

    descriptions of your new home and guardians;

    adjusting to life in the country, especially if it meant getting used to outside toilets, no gas or electricity, etc.;

    how you were accepted by the local community;

    what the new schooling arrangements were;

    feelings of home-sickness.

Case study – Don Coombe

Several hundred of us children boarded the train and set out for the unknown. I suppose the engine driver knew where he was bound, but if he did he wasn't telling. For hour after hour we were shunted and pushed into sidings, across signal points and through little wayside halts, encompassing the whole of the south of England during our marathon journey.

Finally we arrived. Hundreds of us, tired and hungry, were off-loaded onto the crowded station platform at the small Welsh mining and steel town of Abertillery, where we divided into groups of about 50. With an adult leader in charge of each party, we set off, each in a different direction. My little lot climbed a very short steep hill, carrying our few possessions. We hadn't seen hills with such gradients in a town before – it was rather like climbing the side of a house.

There we stood, at the bottom of Clynmawr Street, awaiting selection. Pretty girls were soon mopped up: 'I'll have her,' 'We'll have those two,' and so on. The crowd of us soon diminished. Left on the pavement like a rejected waif was yours truly and my sister Joyce; no one seemed to want boys. Joyce was forced very reluctantly to leave me, but I watched her being taken just a few houses up the street.

At 3 Clynmawr Street lived a very lovely lady, Mrs Clarice Snell, her husband Ernest and their son and daughter – Doug and Clarrie. They were on the doorstep of their house watching the selection process, and when I was left on my own, Doug said to his mother, 'Can't we have him, Mum?' Yes, they had me, and a lifelong friendship began.

Receiving evacuees

It was also strange for those receiving evacuees into their homes and communities. Things to consider include:

- feelings in the community and your house about the imminent deluge of evacuees;
- how much notice you received and how much choice you had about how many children/adults you were to house;
- the financial and ration implications of the enlarged household;
- first impressions of the dishevelled, tired and possibly unruly influx of evacuees;
- the difficulty in choosing who to accept;
- how the new lodgers adapted to your way of life;
- how you adjusted to their manners and attitudes.

Case study – Joy Kennedy

The children all arrived one day and were unloaded at the village hall. It was awful and I felt so sorry for them. All these children, some quite small, taken away from their mums and dads and bundled on to trains to take them to their destination. There they all stood, togged up like parcels, labelled, wearing their best clothes and little hand-knitted pixie hats. Gas mask boxes hung on them.

Those villagers who had agreed to have one or two were in the hall, and the 'pick your evacuee' session took place. They often haggled over the most presentable ones, and any sickly-looking or dirty children were left till last. Younger ones were frightened and bewildered, older ones were angry and decided to make themselves very difficult so that they would be sent home again. As I was so young, I was rather frightened by it all and not convinced that the same thing wouldn't happen to me.

Nearly all the children had to be deloused, and we had never heard so much swearing and bad language before. There was a lot of bed-wetting, naturally, with such upheaval, and complaints of thieving and smelliness from these children from the slums and back-streets of our large cities. Most had never seen green fields, let alone cows and sheep – knives and forks were new to some. There was quite a lot of friction.

The phoney war

Even if evacuation was encouraged, many people chose to stay put, or perhaps drifted back home after a few weeks as the 'phoney war' unfolded. However, life was changing fast with many adjustments to be made.

Case study – Don Buss

People were filling sandbags and placing them in front of police stations and public buildings to stop blast damage from the bombing that was expected. Road signs were also being taken down to confuse the enemy in case of invasion. The wider roads into Thanet had a pole erected each side, supporting a wire about 18ft high. These were spaced every 100 yards or so to stop the Germans using them as landing strips for their planes. Ramsgate airport was also criss-crossed with poles and wire for the same purpose.

The blackout was also introduced, households hurriedly making sure that no light escaped. Very heavy curtains were hung and shutters erected. The windows were covered every four inches or so with inch bands of brown adhesive paper to stop the glass shattering too much.

Anderson and Morrison shelters were also issued; the latter was a heavy sheet of metal about six foot by five foot, supported by heavy angle iron on the corners. This table was about three feet high with wire mesh around three sides. These shelters were designed for use inside the house.

We were given an Anderson shelter which was made out of galvanised iron sheets, shaped and bolted together at the top and with two fitted ends. You could either stand this outside or sink it in the ground and cover it with soil from the hole. We chose the latter and fitted a door so that it was quite cosy and could accommodate about eight people if needed. Condensation was a problem inside the shelter so we painted the interior walls and then threw a liberal coating of sawdust on the paint before it dried.

The Blitz

The phoney war ended abruptly in April 1940 with the aerial bombardment by the Luftwaffe. Over 40,000 people lost their lives – half of them in London – and many more were injured and left homeless.

Case study – Joan Hassall

The raid soon began and the gunfire was frightening. There were more guns, heavier guns and everything was more sharp and intense – a slight lull and then on again, seemingly closer than ever. I was afraid then, dreading what might happen. I was aware of a rushing sound and the feeling of being sucked upwards. I knew it was a bomb falling and it would land very near. Immediately and instinctively I went down on my knees, hands over my head. There came a loud thump, a split second of silence, then the shuddering of the ground beneath and the noise of the explosion and the damage it was causing.

When we came out of the shelter and looked at the back of our house we could see damage to the roof, and all the windows were blown out. Some hats in paper bags that had been on top of the wardrobe in the bedroom were strewn on the garden, as were boxes containing sets of cigarette cards. Inside the house ceilings were down, as was plaster from the walls exposing the wooden laths. Everything was covered in a choking dust. In the living room, the tablecloth and dishes were still on the table, covered in rubble. A cup and saucer was balanced over the edge of the table, held there by a piece of plaster. It was obvious we couldn't stay there.

Freda was in tears. She was going to get married on Whit Monday and her wedding dress was hanging in a cupboard upstairs. She was afraid to go up to get it. I could see that the staircase had moved, but I thought that as I was smaller and lighter than her I would risk it. I went very gingerly and found the dress, which was untouched, and carried it out to her.

For some families the results were even more devastating.

Case study – Violet Kentsbeer

One morning while I was on duty I was told to report to Matron. I began to wonder what I had done wrong, but I could not think what. A terrible shock was in store for me – my mother and two sisters had been badly injured during the night in an air raid. No, it was not an enemy bomb, but a shell from our own guns in the park. I was given immediate release to go home.

My father, being a warden, was out on watch. My mother and the girls, all on fire watch duty, were out in the porch looking for any incendiary bombs which might fall, when this shell came down in the middle of the road, sending shrapnel in all directions and injuring my family where they stood.

I arrived home to find Dad in shock, as he was the first to witness this terrible scene. I can only imagine what it must have been like for him. We went to the hospital and I shall never forget that sight. Mum was unconscious, Nina was barely alive and Win was in a very bad state. It was Win's 19th birthday. Dad and I stayed all night. At about 4.00 am we were asked to go back to the ward and we watched our darling Nina pass away out of the pain she was in. It was two weeks before her 21st birthday – she had been married just six months.

After months in hospital Mum and Win pulled through. I shall not go into details of the injuries they both suffered; it is too distressing to write about even now ....

The war years – as a youngster

Seeing the war through the eyes of a child provides a valuable social commentary.

Case study – Lil Fulker

Imagine if you can a child of six whose entire world seemed to revolve around her beloved Daddy, and in the space of a day he is summoned away to fight in a war. This was followed by nights disturbed by air raid sirens, and the fear of bombs, enemy invasions, gas masks, and sitting under the kitchen table drinking cocoa and waiting for the 'all clear' to sound. There were also nightmares of being chased by Japanese soldiers with bayonets and the alarming fact that fathers do die, which was brought home to us when the father of a girl at school died.

Growing up during the war years

There were plenty of adventures (and dangers) available for enquiring minds:

- the excitement of watching aerial dogfights, little appreciating the fatal consequences for those involved;
- collecting shrapnel and the inevitable 'swapsies' that followed;
- making lead soldiers from the shrapnel;
- playing in bomb craters;
- salvaging (looting!) and playing in bombed-out houses;
- collecting saucepans, iron railings, bones (for cordite), etc. for the war effort.

Older children who remained in major towns and cities grew up fast, not least because of the duties they performed.

Case study – Travers Johnson

As a result of my scout training and my particular interest in First Aid, I realised that I could be of service and decided to join the ARP (Air Raid Precautions). However the minimum age was 16 and even that was only for a messenger ... I was 15. As many volunteers were needed, I filled in the form, ticking 'Wardens Section'... and in the year of my birth the pen accidentally blotted!

We were each required to do a duty turn from 8.00 pm to 6.00 am twice a week. If we had had a particularly bad night I might sleep in, but on the whole I do not remember missing much school. It was quite likely that I would be able to catch up on my sleep in the school air raid shelters during the day raids if we had an alert.

During the latter half of the term electricity was often off, more windows at school were blown in and further structural damage was inflicted on the school building. There was considerable disruption to public transport, and also much time was spent in the shelters. All in all, the amount of actual schoolwork and studying done must have been minimal.

Food

Thanks to rationing, all sorts of new food became part of the nation's diet:

- whale meat;
- snoek;
- spam;
- *National Household* dried milk;

- blended chocolate;
- mock banana – the principle ingredient being mashed parsnip;
- dried egg;
- Woolton pie (Lord Woolton being the Minister of Food).

'Potato Pete' was extolling the virtues of the spud, encouraging housewives to serve more to fill up the family, so saving on other food. Nothing was to be wasted, the boiled potato-water even being advocated as the useful foundation for a soup.

At least a decent, if basic, meal could always be bought in a British Restaurant, and Winston Churchill refused to countenance fish and chips being put on ration.

To supplement meagre rations, flowerbeds, lawns and even window boxes were sacrificed in order to grow food. Chickens and rabbits were kept, and many people were instructed to rear pigs … sometimes rearing an extra one illegally for the family!

Case study – Don Buss

Ordinary folk took on allotments and joined a pig club, where they saved any waste to be collected for the pig. There would be as many as 8–12 people in these clubs. When it was time, they used to get the local butcher to slaughter and cure it. This boosted the rations for some time.

A lot of bartering went on – if you had a surplus of apples in your garden, you would swap some for half a dozen eggs or some potatoes. We also bottled a lot of surplus fruit, made prunes and dried apple rings. It was quite amazing how the most common of fruit or vegetables could be turned into a delicious dish by enterprising housewives of the day. Allotment soup became a favourite recipe for the winter, and we were encouraged to collect rose hips from the hedgerows. These were then turned into rose hip syrup, a very good form of vitamin C for young children.

Rationing

The ration book became the most important household document, but being entitled to certain amounts of food did not mean that you got them – it just depended what the shopkeeper had in stock. Long queues were a common sight, people often joining them without even knowing what they were queuing for.

Case study – Violet Kentsbeer

We were allowed one orange a month and one packet of dried egg powder (the equivalent of a dozen eggs) every eight weeks. Mum was thin and 'didn't like eggs' or anything else much. I read somewhere that a mother is someone who, knowing that there are six people and only five pies for dinner, remarks that she's never much cared for pies – that about sums up my mum. I actually liked the yellow dried egg that we reconstituted with water and scrambled or fried into flat omelettes.

Rationing was in force for a total of 14 years, finally ending in 1954 … nine years after the end of the war! Table 2 shows the sorts of goods that became scare during the war and afterwards. Rations varied throughout the war, being dependent upon supply. Table 3 quotes the lowest 1940 rations, per person per week. Rationing was soon a part of everyday life and pooling resources was commonplace.

Case study – Jean Dudley

By this time Peter and I were considered a couple and we did everything together. Quite often his mother would ask me to Sunday lunch, but as meat was still on ration – even in 1952 – I took along my own chop so that she could cook it with the rest.

Table 2   The length of time common items were rationed, during and after World War II.

Item	First Rationed	De-rationed
Tea	1940	1952
Sugar	1940	1953
Cream	1940	1953
Butter	1940	1954
Meat	1940	1954
Petrol	1940	1950
Shell eggs	1941	1953
Cheese	1941	1954
Clothes	1941	1949
Jam	1941	1948
Sweets	1942	1953
Bread	1946	1948

Table 3   Ration allocation (by weight or monetary value).

Bacon and ham	4oz
Sugar	8oz
Tea	2oz
Meat	1s 10d (9p)
Butter	2oz
Cheese	1oz
Margarine	4oz
Cooking fats	2oz

The black market

During the war – and afterwards – the black market flourished, and it was always worth keeping on the right side of the butcher and grocer in case anything was available 'under the counter'.

Case study – Helmut Rothenberg

On one of my regular visits to Keighley, well after the war had finished but while rationing was still in existence, Peter asked whether I would like to take some eggs home. At that time we had four children and I knew that Annema would be delighted with some eggs. During the evening Peter and I went to a local farmer, who was pleased to help us pack each egg – there must have been a couple of hundred – individually into a large suitcase which I had brought along. The sale of eggs was controlled and the farmer was only allowed to sell them at a fixed price to the Ministry of Food for distribution at their discretion. Therefore any price the farmer could get for additional eggs (and of course it was well inflated) was most favourable for him.

The next day I travelled back to London on the train from Leeds. As was my custom, I gave my luggage to the porter and told him to be very careful when putting the suitcase onto the rack because it had 'instruments' inside. The train started moving and shortly thereafter a waiter from the dining car came into the compartment, inviting the occupants to dinner. I was hesitant and must have looked up at my case. The only other traveller in the compartment, a man sitting opposite me who had read his newspaper and been completely silent until then, smiled and said to me, 'Let's go in and have dinner together … don't worry, I've got eggs in my case too.' Needless to say, I was a very popular chap with both family and friends when I returned to London.

Make-do-and-mend

It was not just food that was rationed; clothing coupons were equally precious. Each person was entitled to 66 coupons a year, and even a woollen shirt or combination required eight coupons for an adult and six for a child. As a result, 'make-do-and-mend' became part of the national vocabulary: worn sheets were turned side to middle, coats were made from blankets, anything that could be darned was, and strips were inserted into skirts to lengthen them as children grew older. A silk parachute being acquired (no questions asked) was unheard-of luxury.

Case study – Lil Fulker

I remember in detail the clothes we used to wear during the war years. We had lace-up shoes, navy blue knickers, and liberty bodices with rubber buttons which melted and felt sticky if you washed them in water that was too hot. Our knitted dark woollen socks were kept up by home-made elastic garters which left patterns round our legs because they were invariably too tight. Sometimes we wore brown woollen stockings that wrinkled round our legs.

When wool was on coupons, Mum once commented that we girls needed new vests but she had no wool with which to knit them. We all filtered upstairs, ostensibly to play, and came down some time later with smiling faces and an outsize ball of wool which we had obtained by unravelling all the blanket stitching meant to prevent the blankets from fraying round the edges! It was only one- or two-ply so was totally unsuitable for knitting, but Mum did not have the heart to tell us off.

News of the war

You might recall following the course of the war on the wireless, perhaps also having a map pinned on the wall. Wireless broadcasts, cinema newsreels and newspapers were censored to protect morale and to ensure that sensitive information was not passed into the hands of the enemy. Everyone was made aware that 'Careless talk costs lives', and people were encouraged to 'be like Dad, keep mum!'

Letters home from servicemen were vetted by the censor's pen, and as a result it was difficult to know the whereabouts of loved ones.

Case study – Joan Belk

We knew that Ernest was being sent overseas because when we last saw him he had been issued with pith helmet, puttees, etc. We didn't hear a word from him for three weeks, and Mum and Dad were very worried, avidly listening to any news from the high seas. Then, one teatime, while we were eating, in walked Ernest. We all had tears in our eyes. 'Oh, where have you been Son?' asked Dad. 'At Greasborough, Dad,' my brother answered, 'On the "Ack-Ack" guns.' This was only about three miles away. When we realised what had happened, we saw the funny side of it and laughed and laughed. The war was on, mail had been stopped in case any word got to the enemy, and we were very spy-conscious in those days.

American GIs

The Japanese attack on Pearl Harbour in December 1941 brought the Americans into the war. Their presence boosted morale, but there were wider-reaching consequences as the cultural landscape of Britain changed. The Americans were loved by some (often literally!), but were not welcomed by all.

Cast study – Joy Kennedy

What a difference the Americans made to us children. Suddenly we had these friendly, outgoing types in snazzy uniforms walking around our streets. We soon found that they carried a constant supply of 'candy' and chewing gum which they generously handed out to us. Their camp stores (PX) supplied cigarettes, nylon stockings to replace the long-forgotten silk ones, scented soap and chocolate. Their bases were treasure houses of luxuries, as well as things new to British life – we also thought their way of speaking was so strange.

I also loved the Christmas parties the Americans gave – I had never been to anything quite like it. There was so much food, jelly and ice cream, and the hall was so pretty with the streamers and balloons. The games were fun and the prizes out of this world … real dolls, for instance. The Christmas tree was huge, right up to the ceiling and covered with sparkling tinsel, large, brightly coloured baubles and lots of lights. There was also a real Santa, with a sack full of great big toys, one for each of us, clearly marked with our names. Yes, I enjoyed the Americans coming to our village, but I believe mothers of older girls, and husbands away in the Forces, were not so thrilled!

On the lighter side

The entertainment industry played a very important part in keeping up morale.

Radio

Case study – Ron Larkin

ITMA on the BBC Light Programme was a British institution during the war. Tommy Handley was already established as a comedian in 1939, though not what would be called a household name. *ITMA* – It's That Man Again – was originally a reference to Adolf Hitler, but it soon became so much a part of the wartime scene that its mere name seems to evoke a memory of the blacked-out living room at 8.30 on a Sunday evening with, perhaps, even a siren wailing in the distance.

The whole show originally centred around Tommy Handley playing a succession of weird characters – such as the 'Minister of Aggravations and Mysteries', working in the 'Office of Twerps' and coping with the persistent disapproval of the hidebound Civil Servant, 'Fusspot'. He also created a German character called 'Funf', who would continually interrupt him on the phone – beginning by saying, 'This is Funf calling.' This became a national saying, with people ridiculing the German language. One of the most famous characters was the charlady, 'Mrs Mopp', with her soon-immortal question, which was probably the most risqué question that you would hear on the BBC then – 'Can I do you now, Sir?'

Cinema

Films and film stars, songs and singers also played their part in keeping up morale. You are sure to have your own favourites, and the history notes section will also help, but here are a few to start with:

- the 'Road' films with Bing Crosby, Bob Hope and Dorothy Lamour;
- Casablanca with Humphrey Bogart and Ingrid Bergman;
- the all-time blockbuster Gone with the Wind with Clark Gable and Vivienne Leigh;
- Walt Disney was doing his bit with Pinocchio, Dumbo, Bambi and Fantasia.

Songs

If certain songs stir strong memories, you might like to include them. Songs associated with the war include:

- We're Gonna Hang Out the Washing on the Siegfried Line;
- White Cliffs of Dover;
- We'll Meet Again;
- Run Rabbit;
- Meet Me in the Blackout;
- You Can't Blackout the Moon.

Miscellany

Other areas likely to spark a few memories include:

- sleeping in the London Underground or out in the countryside;
- conscientious objectors;
- siren suits, as worn by Winston Churchill;
- making handbags out of gas mask boxes;
- *Silktona* 'liquid silk stockings'… or perhaps it was gravy or coffee on the legs, with the 'seam' being drawn with an eyeliner pencil;
- the luxury of real stockings and having them repaired at 4d per inch when they laddered;
- women wearing trousers for the first time;
- the morale-boosting rhetoric and rousing speeches of Winston Churchill;
- Lord Haw-Haw, and Oswald Mosely and his blackshirts;
- constantly being aware of loved-ones serving in the war and dreading the knock on the door from the police;
- D-Day and the feeling that victory was just around the corner;
- the way the war dragged on, particularly towards the end.

The V1 and V2

After D-Day and the assault on mainland Europe, there was optimism that the war would soon end. However, it dragged on for many more months, during which a new threat was seen over the skies of Britain. June 1944 saw the first V1 cross the Channel, flames spurting from its tail. These flying bombs, or 'doodlebugs' as they soon became known, carried just enough fuel to reach their destinations. When the engine cut out, it was a matter of seconds before the explosion followed. As if these were not frightening enough, in September 1944 the first V2s were launched. These rockets, with one ton of explosives in the warheads, were silent so gave no warning of their approach. If you witnessed either of these weapons, describe them and the fear they instilled.

The end of the war

VE-Day was on Tuesday 8 May 1945, with VJ-Day following on 15 August. After six long years of war, try to describe:

- when you felt that the war was finally over – VE-Day, VJ-Day, when loved ones returned … if they did;
- your feelings – euphoria, emptiness, sadness, loss, relief, or whatever it was;
- any partying or street parties;
- your thoughts on the past six years;
- your hopes for the future;
- your reflections on how things had changed forever.

Case study – Joan Joyce

On VE-Day, and again on VJ-Day, everybody breathed a huge sigh of relief. Then there was a big celebration when the lights of London were switched on after all the years of darkness and gloom. Zoe Gail did the honours, and it was wonderful when the whole place was suddenly ablaze. People spontaneously broke out into, *When the Lights Go On Again* and the crowd roared! It was an exciting time and one I wouldn't have missed – it was indeed a rare moment.

Demobilisation

Even after victory had been celebrated there were still some mop-ping-up operations in which lives were lost, and it was many months or even a couple of years before everyone was demobilised. Those who had not seen their loved ones for several years were sometimes in for a shock.

Case study – Joan Hassall

In the autumn of 1945 we heard that Dad was coming home from Gibraltar and would be arriving at Liverpool, the port he had left from in 1941. After he was demobbed he travelled down to Plymouth by train, and Mum asked me to meet him at the station so she could have everything ready at home. I was excited to be having him home again and dressed up for the occasion – I wore my green suit that I was fond of. My hair was shoulder-length and done in a more mature style, high at the front and sides and the rest falling as loose curls. I liked wearing earrings, and I also used light make-up and lipstick since starting work.

Waiting on the platform as the train arrived, I remember the doors opening and lots of people getting off, struggling with luggage and passing me as I tried to pick out my father. In the distance, I saw him coming towards me with the two men he had gone out with. I hurried to him, stopped and said 'Dad'. I could tell by the look on his face that he hadn't recognised me, but after a moment and a hug and a kiss he got over the shock. Dad had no idea how I had grown up.

The aftermath

Few people were left untainted by the war.

Case study – Joy Kennedy

It did not take long for the euphoria of victory to be replaced with counting the cost. Everyone was tired and the country and relationships had to be rebuilt. Many wives had not seen their husbands for years, but people had changed and frequently the reunions were fraught with difficulties. The years of separation had caused people to grow apart, and women had become far more independent as a result of having to manage alone and cope with whatever came along, many of them also having been to work and having enjoyed receiving their own wage.

Young children did not know their fathers, and this included my brother. They would resent this man telling them what to do, or worse, being reprimanded by him and want him to go away. They had grown used to living without him. It was to take quite a period of readjustment for many homes.

Neither husband nor wife could understand fully what each had been through. A photograph had replaced the presence of a real man about the house. Some wives had been unfaithful, which caused much heartbreak. In some cases there were even children fathered by another man.

Points to ponder

- What are your overall impressions of the war years?
- What did your parents feel about the war?
- How did the war alter people's values and expectations?

Top tips

- Write down everything initially; you can always cut it out later if you want to. However, often the smallest details are the most fascinating, and the fact that you remember them after 40, 50, 60+ years must mean something. If your grandmother had written a book, you would surely want to know everything. It will be the same with your book, so write it down.

- Leave a notepad by the bed, for when that stray thought pops into your head just before you nod off.

The War Years – Part II: Serving the Nation

8

Having looked at the upheaval imposed on Britain during the war, we now consider some of the ways in which people served their country. Whilst only a small selection can be provided, most people who served in some capacity will be able to identify with elements of the first-hand accounts.

Home defence

In May 1940 the War Minister, Anthony Eden, appealed for volunteers to defend Britain in case of invasion. The following day 250,000 men had come forward, many of them veterans of The Great War. Initially known as Local Defence Volunteers, or the 'LDV', they were renamed the Home Guard by Winston Churchill, who ensured that by the winter of 1940 they had uniforms and rifles … even if they were First World War issue. Despite being endearingly called 'Dad's Army' and later immortalised in the TV series of that name, the Home Guard undertook dangerous work like bomb disposal and manning ack-ack guns – indeed, over 1,200 died in service.

A host of other services also required volunteers, including Air Raid Wardens, rescue workers, first aid workers and ambulance drivers, the Auxiliary Fire Service with their army of firewatchers, and the Women's Royal Volunteer Service dispensing comfort and endless mugs of tea.

If you or a member of your family were involved in any voluntary capacity, it is likely that you will have plenty of stories to relate.

Conscription

The National Service (Armed Forces) Act, passed on the outbreak of war, made all able-bodied men between the ages of 18 and 41 available for conscription. Those in 'reserved' occupations, like mining, farming and other industries essential to the war effort, were exempt. Indeed, such was the increased demand for coal during the war, that by December 1943 'Bevin Boys' were required, one man in every ten conscripts under the age of 25 being sent down the pits.

Whether you volunteered or were conscripted, you might like to record which service you wanted to join and the type of work you aspired to … and how this matched the reality.

Case study – Phyl Jackson

By the beginning of 1942 I was getting restless in my dull office job with *Legal and General*. One after another of the young men joined up or were conscripted and I began to feel that perhaps I too should be contributing more to the war effort – besides, I felt I should like to choose what I did before I got drafted into something disagreeable. Women faced conscription along with men by that time.

Having perused the brochures of all three services, I chose the WAAF, with a view to training as a wireless operator. This ambition was soon to be dashed, for on application I was told the trade was at present fully subscribed. I never questioned this at the time, but now realise that other trades probably needed pushing. I had the choice of being a cook, a driver, a clerk or a general aircraft hand – not perhaps an exciting prospect. Cooking for the masses didn't appeal, driving even less so. I was already used to clerical work, so that seemed the obvious choice. At least it wouldn't be any more boring than the work I was already doing, I told myself …

If you joined up describe:

-   what sort of send-off you received, if any;
-   what your thoughts were – gung-ho, excited, nervous, frightened, etc.;
-   any interesting stories about the signing-on procedure, especially if you were under-age;
-   how you travelled to your muster point, and any difficulties with 'goodbyes' to loved ones;
-   feelings of homesickness.

First impressions of service life

Joining up and induction into service was quite a culture shock for most. Your writing here might include:

- your number, no doubt indelibly printed on your memory;
- first impressions of your billet and your fellow recruits, and any notable characters;
- the instructors and what you were told by the 'old lags';
- being kitted out, and how the uniform fitted;
- the routine of the first few days, signing countless forms, the haircut, medical, etc.;
- how you adapted to the physical demands of the basic training;
- learning to march, shoot, unarmed combat and what to do in the event of a gas attack;
- what you were good at ... and what you were not so good at;
- what the food was like.

It was not just the men who had to endure the embarrassment of medicals.

Case study – Joan Belk

The next day we had our inoculations, etc., and we were marched to another hut for X-rays. Oh boy, was I embarrassed. We were all lined up, and the woman sergeant shouted, 'All clothes off, except your pants.' As I was very modest, I put my shirt round my shoulders. There was a bellow down my right ear, 'You, Airwoman, shirt off, head up, shoulders back, stomach in.' So I stood there with my hands across my chest. I turned round a bit and looked up the room. I'd never seen so many boobs in my life, talk about big ones, small ones, some as big as your head, as the old song goes, and I felt a lot better as I was average. I always had a sense of humour, so what made me smile to myself was all the pants we wore – Directoire knickers ('passion killers') they were called, made out of silk in Air Force blue with elasticated legs – the ones old ladies wore. Oh boy, did we look a right bunch of 'nanas.

I soon had the smile wiped off my face. The female doctor went for her dinner and a tall, handsome male doctor took over. How I blushed when he said, 'Come along Airwoman, it won't take long,' and then he smiled, which made me blush all the more. 'That didn't hurt, did it?' he said, but I was glad to escape.

More anecdotes regarding basic training can be found in Chapter 10 on National Service.

Training

When it came to the training, it was certainly thorough.

Case study – Travers Johnson

I did my advanced infantry training at The Dale in Chester. The accent was certainly on physical fitness: Monday was a 24-mile route march; Tuesday we 'doubled' about the camp all day; Wednesday was a cross-country run, followed by sports; Thursday, ten miles in two hours, dress battle order and rifle; Friday it was doubling about the camp again all day, and Saturday was the Battalion Sergeant Major's drill parade. Then, if we were lucky, it was off home for a short break. This was all part of Montgomery's toughening-up policy and was the same throughout the Army for all ranks.

Army infantry training was designed to make the soldier capable of looking after himself in any tough situation – unarmed combat training was certainly a great morale booster in that respect. During fieldcraft training we were taught to be able to move quickly and quietly, and know how not to be seen or heard. We were given training in how to walk either outside or inside a building in the dark, without falling over our feet, bumping into anything or making a noise. It is quite incredible how quietly it is possible to move and walk when you know how!

I also learnt to live, cook and eat well, whatever the situation. This type of training gave one great confidence later in civilian life. There were very few circumstances, pleasant or very unpleasant, where I felt I was not in complete command of the situation – this, I am sure, was due to such thorough training.

War service

A selection of experiences follow in the hope that some might strike a chord.

High excitement

Case study – Jim Goode

I went to Wandsworth Jail to collect the prisoner. John was a safe-cracker pure and simple; he had not given any trouble nor indulged in any violence. He agreed to the terms of our arrangement – in return for successfully helping on our assignment, he would gain his freedom.

The next morning we were briefed regarding the job. We were to be dropped in France near a château being used as a German signals headquarters. We were to parachute in at night, make our way to the château and break in. After locating the room where the signals safe was kept, John was to open it, photograph the contents and replace them. If disturbed, we would take the contents with us, close the safe, make our way to a pick-up point some 30 miles away and wait until picked up by an aircraft. It was pointed out that it would be preferable if this mission could be accomplished without any traces being left, so that the enemy would be unaware that we knew the contents of the safe.

(The mission was successfully accomplished.)

The idyllic

Case study – Roy Barton

In Athens the sky seemed to be eternally blue; the sun shone and life was not only pleasant, it was exhilarating. I even played for the RAF football team against a Greek XI in the national stadium … never mind the result. With so much time on our hands, I sent home for my tennis racquet and all the trimmings, and had actually received them. At this time I was prone to remark: 'If this is war, may it go on forever.'

Professional judgement

Leonard Hall, prisoner of war in Stalag Luft 3, writes about the part he played in what has become known as 'The Great Escape'.

Case study – Leonard Hall

On the morning of Friday 24 March 1944, I was asked by a member of the Escape Committee to provide a weather forecast. I asked for, and was allowed, 15 minutes or so to walk round the circuit and glean what I could from the sky and the wind conditions. Needless to say, no weather maps were available and I could only draw on my knowledge of weather patterns, cloud formations, wind speeds and directions. I knew Roger Bushell was seeking cloud to obscure the starlight and whatever little moonlight there might have been, and wind to drown the noise. I went to his room, where various senior members of the Escape Committee were gathered, and said that I thought there was a very good chance of such conditions that night. 'Right,' said Roger, 'We go tonight.' The weather undoubtedly played an important part in the decision, but I guess Bushell wanted to go that night or very soon after, because of the risk of discovery. He would not have wanted to wait through another full moon period. Despite the making of bricks without straw, the forecast did prove remarkably accurate.

Once the decision was taken, the whole highly complex escape operation swung into action. Although my name had gone into the hat for one of the escape places remaining after the well-earned priorities had been allocated, it had not been drawn out. It was simply up to all of us who were not directly involved to carry on normal camp activities so that the Germans should not know that anything unusual was afoot. I remember in particular taking one of my meteorology classes, with a much smaller attendance than usual, and clearly, although of course not a word could be said, neither lecturer nor students had their minds on the job!

That evening, all the potential escapers donned their escape gear – some 220 in all, of whom 70 were top priority cases – and collected forged passes, money, compasses, food and maps. Block 104 was cleared to make room for all the escapers. I remember being one of the last to leave 104 because I had gone round turning taps on and off and making a noise to give the impression of normality. Then I moved over to 120 to which I had been assigned and went to bed and to sleep ... or did I? There was a lot to think about.

Soon after dawn there was a shot – a guard had stumbled on the exit into the woods and the alarm was raised. The number of escapers was disappointing. It transpired that there had been an air raid on Berlin. The perimeter lights went out and so did the lights in the tunnel, and no more than 80 had got out when the alarm was raised. The last four were picked up as they came out of the tunnel, which left 76. Of the others, 15 were brought back to the camp to spend their 30 days in the cooler – which, according to the Geneva Convention, is what should have happened to all those recaptured – eight were sent to concentration camps such as Sachsenhausen. If you want to know more, please read *Moonless Night* by Jimmy James. As the world knows, 50 were shot, murdered, apparently on the personal order of Hitler. Three were brilliant and fortunate enough to get home – Jens Muller, Per Bergsland, both Norwegians, and Bob Van der Stok, a Dutchman. All three, of course, had total command of a second European language.

Working in the land army

> ### Case study – Pat Nickson (writing a letter)
>
> My job consists of the milk round. I drive an *Austin* van and tootle about Kendal armed with hundreds of bottles and a can to measure. I rather enjoy it really, for you've no idea what goes on behind the scenes! After the war I shall write a book called, say, 'Memoirs of a Milkmaid', or, 'Autobiography of a milk bottle'. There is a great deal of social service in the job – for not only do I deliver a pint here and a quart there, but I also … er … hold the baby … watch the bacon … instruct a newly-wed on how to make pastry … and wash numerous milk jugs. One meets all types: there are high brows and low brows, some houses that are the last word in perfection, and others where one has to take a deep breath and hold it all the time.

The unusual

Case study – Joan Belk

We arrived at Gosport only to be told by the sergeant, 'I think you've got the wrong place, we don't have WAAFs on this squadron – they're all men.' We had got there before the report about us had arrived, but I had our papers. Looking shocked, the sergeant said, 'Women flight mechanics; I didn't know there were any. Let's see what you can do.' With a grin on his face, he shouted to one of the lads, 'Jones, this is your new oppo, Jacko.'

I nearly fainted when I saw the planes were *Lancasters*. As I was only five foot four and about eight stone, the wheels were nearly as big as me. It was a good job that heights didn't bother me – the thought of being up there (they are almost as big as a house) could make me faint now.

When I had finished, I sat in the cockpit and sized up the panel – there seemed to be hundreds of gauges. Dad had taught me to simplify things, so in my mind I imagined that there were only two engines, not four, and then classed them as two *Spitfire* engines. I looked through the window and shouted 'All clear,' and 'All clear' came back.

I helped my oppo do his engines by taking the covers off, putting them on the ground and seeing that everything was all clear. When we had finished, we went in to sign and the sergeant asked how I'd done. 'OK,' said my oppo, 'I think she knows more than me. By the way, what kites have you been on, Jacko?' I replied, 'Spitfires.' They were astonished. 'Spitfires' was a magical word, everybody loved them, and so we were accepted. They were very friendly and helped us a lot.

Making crucial decisions

Case study – Group Captain Guy Bolland

The pilots based permanently at Gibraltar got used to the variable winds blowing around the Rock, which caused so much trouble in landing. A southerly wind, split by the mass of the Rock, can give air currents from both ends of the runway at once, causing the windsocks at each end to point towards each other. But for young pilots flying out new aircraft and making their first long-distance flight over the sea, landing at Gibraltar was a terrifying task. Not only were all of them getting short of petrol, but every circuit had to be made round the southern end of the Rock, as they were not allowed to fly over Spain. The wrecks of aircraft that had not quite managed to land or take off correctly abounded at both ends of the runway, and these further impaired the confidence of pilots using it.

The reinforcement aircraft arrived in the evenings, having set out from the UK at first light. There might be 20 in the circuit waiting to land, and, because the pilots could not fly at night, if a plane crashed on landing and it could not be moved quickly, I regret to say that I ordered the aircraft to be pushed into the sea by bulldozer. Had I not, as a matter of policy, decided on this action, I might on any one evening have lost many machines, either due to shortage of fuel or by keeping the pilots waiting in a long circuit, building up a high state of nervousness which would cause more crashes. I tried to be on the runway in person every evening when the UK aircraft were arriving because split-second decisions had to be made. Air traffic control was a major worry, quite apart from the obvious problem of having airfield construction work in progress all the time.

In the build-up to Torch, General Dwight Eisenhower made many visits to the airfield in the evenings when the UK aircraft were due to arrive, and as Station Commander I used to accompany him whilst he was on the airfield. He was a charming man and, of course, most interested in all that was going on, witnessing several of the crashes on landing. Very quickly he realised that when we had a crash, with 20 to 30 aircraft in the circuit and nowhere to which they could be diverted, it was essential to clear the runway within minutes, and if the crash happened to be on the extension there was no option but to push the aircraft into the water.

When General Montgomery heard what I was doing, sometimes to Army co-operation aircraft intended for his HQ, without understanding the circumstances, he complained in no uncertain terms to the Air Ministry that there was a madman called Bolland at Gibraltar who was bulldozing new aircraft into the water without any effort being made to salvage them! He needed those aircraft urgently in the desert and wanted me removed immediately! Fortunately, General Eisenhower knew very well what I was doing, and why, and I heard no more from Montgomery. Instead of being sacked, as a very young officer I was awarded the CBE, and I can only believe that this was on the recommendation of Eisenhower.

The mundane

Case study – Phyl Jackson

The girls we had met on the first evening in Gloucester had not exaggerated the tedium of the records work. We were set to type nominal rolls ad nauseam on ancient *Olivetti* machines that did not even have a standard keyboard – as a touch typist I found it most frustrating. A mere nine days in, we heard a rumour that our job was to stop. It did, but instead we were put on to the even more boring task of checking the nominal rolls. By comparison, checking insurance renewal notices seemed, in retrospect, quite an intellectual exercise.

The heat of battle

Case study – Travers Johnson in the Peel Marshes

We finally advanced to our position and dug in quickly on the forward slope overlooking the village of Liesel with its commanding church spire. We were persistently machine-gunned, mortared and shelled by German artillery – the especially sharp crack of the 88s was most unwelcome. It was here that an 88 shell dropped rather too near me and from which my hearing troubles began.

We had to do two hours on guard and two off all through the night, plus stand-to at dawn. Then we shot-in a full-scale attack from our front line positions early morning – what with the noise of the artillery from both sides, smoke and fumes from bursting shells and from burning buildings and ricks, then the large numbers of tanks which had formed up starting to advance through our dug-in *Vickers*, the adrenalin really started to work.

In an attack situation, the tank crews had their protective steel visors down and so driver visibility was severely restricted – the thought of a 30-ton *Churchill* tank running over one's slit trench is not a pleasant one. We had found that the best means of attracting the attention of tank drivers was to stand up in the trench and slowly wave a shovel. This was a simple, but very, very effective way of drawing attention to our positions ... hoping of course that we were not shot in the process by an enemy bullet!

Over the following days and weeks, the attack progressed through the Peel Marshes. Being in the bogs was bad enough, but when it rained continuously for days the situation became unbelievable. After each attack we consolidated, forming 'strong points' and dug in as per battle routine, only to wake up in the middle of the night to find ourselves sitting, or worse, lying in three-plus inches of water that had seeped into our slit trench. It was very dangerous and virtually impossible, when in the front line of an active attack situation, to move any distance at night. We just had to stay put and survive. How we all never had double pneumonia, living in cold wet clothes for weeks, I shall never know.

Making the best of any leave

Case study – Phyl Jackson

Forty-eight hour passes and leaves came round more rarely, but 36 hour ones could be had most weekends unless one was on duty. What bliss it was to get out of uniform into my own clothes and hairstyle (especially important considerations at that stage). To sleep in a bed that needed no stacking and have a lie-in if I wanted, instead of rising at 6.30 am, were other joys, as was home cooking.

Three of us with a 36 hour pass were intending to hitch-hike, but on the way we collected three more girls, which made our chances of getting lifts almost impossible. We hadn't got further than North Leach when it got dark, and we decided to split up. I contemplated spending the night in a haystack, until I saw a rat run across it. We managed a lift to a transport café at High Wycombe and I felt I was near enough home to continue, leaving the others there. I had twelve miles to walk in the dark and was getting sleepier all the time. There was also an air raid warning as I went through Beaconsfield, but luckily no action. I'll always remember the scent of the flowers in the June air. A lorry picked me up just outside Uxbridge and I arrived home at 4.40 am. Mum had given up expecting me of course. I had to return to Gloucester the same evening, but a few hours' freedom had been worth it.

Prisoners of war

Case study – Leonard Hall

I was more than depressed to find myself at Wilhelmshaven, the Navy interrogation centre, and more days, indeed weeks, of solitary confinement and, from the German point of view, unproductive interrogation. Solitary confinement was a traumatic experience engendering brooding and self-pity, but I did not let my morale sink beyond recall. The saying, 'Think positive, and do not become depressed,' was never more important, or harder to achieve.

I remember a guard coming into my room on 25 February 1943, to find me singing. 'Why do you sing?' he asked me, with incredulity in his voice. 'It's my birthday!' I replied. I am sure the guard thought I was even more mad than most mad Englishmen! My memory is not very clear about how I did spend my time – setting myself mental puzzles, and I remember getting hold of enough paper, or was it card, to create 52 playing cards to play patience. It was the other kind of patience that was required!

When transferred to Stalag Luft 3, my philosophy, and it was most people's philosophy, was that you had to keep busy – whether you were going to lectures, playing football, giving lectures, digging tunnels, performing on the stage, or whatever you were doing, you had to look at your diary and say, 'Sorry, I can't do that on Friday, I have a prior engagement.' If you were in that situation you were all right, because the morale in the camp was very good and very high. There were just a few people, who lay on their bunks waiting for the war to end, who deteriorated. There were not many of them.

Being a prisoner of war for two and a half years was a highly educational experience, from which I claim to have emerged knowing all there was to know about men, and nothing at all about women.

The end of the war

> ### *Case study – Travers Johnson*
>
> We finished the campaign at Volksdorf just outside Hamburg. The official news that fighting had stopped was given to us by the Company Quartermaster on his daily visit with our essential supplies, rations and post. Ours was his first call and I was at HQ when he came in through the door and said, 'It's all over, official.' I can distinctly remember a young soldier who had recently arrived as a replacement throwing his hat in the air and dancing around shouting with glee. He was told in no uncertain terms to shut up and clear out or else. We just sat or stood there quietly – nobody spoke. Tears rolled down Badger's weather-beaten face as relief dawned upon him and us that we had survived. We quietly remembered those who had not. We were a very quiet and subdued platoon that evening.

Demobilisation

As well as recording the logistics of demobilisation and your clothing entitlement, you might also like to write about your feelings:

- elated about going home;
- frustrated about the interminable delays;
- wary about what the future held;
- deflated about missing all the camaraderie and the adrenalin-filled life you had been leading;
- concern about rebuilding family life.

It will also be interesting to observe what happened to these expectations and how your feelings altered once you had been home a few months.

Points to ponder

- How did the war years change you?
- What opportunities did the war open up for you?
- What course might your life have followed without a war?

Top tips

- Acronyms and abbreviations abound in military circles. The usual practice is to write the full title on the first occasion, followed by the short version in brackets. Thereafter the acronym or abbreviation may be used.

- Many of your readers may not be familiar with military terms and titles. If several are used in your writing, it may be worth including a glossary.

National Service

9

Whilst this chapter concentrates on National Service after the war, it is recommended that it be viewed in conjunction with Chapter 8 as some of those case studies might also strike a chord. Whether enjoyed or endured, National Service invariably evokes a multitude of stories for those who went in as boys and emerged as men.

Background

National Service commenced after the war, taking over from conscription; it continued until the end of 1960 although the upper age limit was reduced to 25. The original length of service of one year was increased to 18 months in December 1948, and then to two years with the outbreak of the Korean War in 1950. Exemptions for reserved occupations continued.

The Royal Navy stopped taking national servicemen in the early 1950s, and whilst many raw recruits might have had visions of joining the Royal Air Force, by far the majority found themselves in the Army.

There is a tendency for the value of National Service, especially in the 1950s, to be belittled; however, men served alongside the regulars throughout the world and 400 or so lost their lives. Along with postings in conflict areas like Malaya, Korea, Palestine, Kenya, Cyprus and Suez, many national servicemen served in countries that were gaining their independence from the British Empire.

Joining up

Describe your feelings about National Service.

✍ You might have been looking forward to getting away from home, relishing the excitement of what was in store, seeing the world and living a bit.

✍ If you had led a sheltered life, perhaps you were apprehensive about the rough types you would undoubtedly encounter. Relate any stories you heard in advance, and how exaggerated they were in reality.

✍ Perhaps you saw National Service as an inconvenience, preventing you from getting on with your career or studies. If you had the option of deferring your National Service, what choice did you make and why?

✍ Did you use the experience of National Service to your advantage, like learning to type, drive, lecture or some other skill useful in later life?

   ☩ Did you try to avoid National Service on medical, compassionate, political or religious grounds, or on some pretext? Maybe you considered an alternative to National Service, like joining the police or the merchant navy?

Basic training

If you experienced basic training it is unlikely that there will be any shortage of stories, not least how you prepared for the inspection party:

   ☩ using a heated spoon or fork handle, or perhaps an iron, to smooth out the dimples on the toecaps and heels of your boots … then the endless hours of bull until you could see the reflection of your face in the shine;

   ☩ perhaps paying someone to do this for you – invariably someone had a knack for it, and might be open to the offer of a few extra fags;

   ☩ blancoing belts and webbing;

   ☩ taking an eternity to make your bed so that it was perfectly square, then carefully laying the pack on top;

   ☩ leaving squares of old blankets by the door to 'skate' over the floor in an effort to protect the hard-won shine;

   ☩ ensuring the window was spotless if you were unlucky enough to have your bed next to one.

Then, of course, came the actual inspection.

Case study – Ron Larkin in RAF

The Wing Commander stood aloof at the head of the inspection party – you could almost see his brain planning what devious move to make – when suddenly he took the white china mug from the bedside locker nearest to him. Without even looking inside the mug, he held it out at arm's length, declaring it to be 'verminous' and just let it drop to the floor, smashing it into a dozen pieces. Not a sound was made by anyone, but our anguish was palpable. The dropping of the mug was not only unnecessary, but also a callous act as the mugs were, surprisingly, not supplied by the RAF but had to be purchased by each airman from the NAAFI. Whilst made of good quality china, they cost 2/6 representing 10% of our weekly allowance – and the last thing you needed was some officer wasting your money. About three more mugs suffered the same fate; one airman's razor was thrown on the floor and one of the inspection party 'accidentally' trod on it, rendering it unusable.

Halfway along the hut the Wing Commander declared that 'This hut is a disaster. The inspection is being abandoned and a further inspection will be made tomorrow.' We all felt not only totally humiliated and distraught, but also very angry and slightly frightened. Having spent so much time and hard work the previous night, we didn't know what we could do differently for the hut to pass the next inspection.

We were slightly gratified to learn that two of the other huts in the Flight had suffered the same fate, meaning that only one hut out of four had passed the inspection … their turn came the following week!

The parade ground

Learning to march as one took some doing, and early attempts probably brought the forlorn realisation that it was never likely to happen. Describe your parade ground experiences … and the repartee.

Case study – Ron Larkin

Whilst you could not turn your eyes when at attention, you had a very good idea where the Drill Instructor was in relation to your position. Occasionally, however, you could be caught out and be shocked to find him literally breathing down your neck saying, 'Airman, am I 'urting you? '

'No, Sir,' would be your automatic reply, only to be admonished for calling a corporal 'Sir'. The charade would be repeated with you saying, 'No, Corporal,' to which he would bark, 'Well I bloody well ought to be, 'cos I'm standing on your hair – now go and get a bloody 'aircut!'

Of course, the whole Flight would laugh, as the Corporal wanted, only for him to admonish them for their outburst. These drill instructors had countless well-used witticisms with which to ply us all day. Some were quite funny at the first time of hearing, but they palled a little after constant use. Another favourite was: 'Airman, did you use a mirror when you shaved this morning?'
'Yes, Corporal.'
'Well, tomorrow I suggest you use a bloody razor.'

Then there were the punishments meted out for your heinous misdemeanours, not just the doubling up and doing countless press-ups, but also the mind-numbingly tedious tasks:

- ᕦ painting coal white;
- ᕦ cleaning the latrines;
- ᕦ sweeping the parade ground with a toothbrush;
- ᕦ spud bashing – tons of them;
- ᕦ washing hundreds of greasy pots and pans in the 'tin room';
- ᕦ extra drill at night.

Never complaining or volunteering

Any complaints tended to be counter-productive as Joan Belk and her colleagues found to their cost. Whilst they were regulars in the WAAF, any national serviceman will be able to identify with their plight.

Case study – Joan Belk

My three friends and I were having dinner one day, when the Duty Officer came round. 'Any complaints, Airwomen?' he said, smiling at us.

'Yes Sir,' said Lilian, 'we don't like the potatoes looking at us while we are eating.' (She meant the eyes on the potatoes.)

'Right girls,' he said, still smiling, 'report to the cook house at nine o'clock in the morning – you, you, you and you.'

The four of us reported to the smiling Sergeant the next morning. He ordered us to follow him, and I was thinking, 'Why is he smiling?' I soon found out.

'There you are girls,' he said, handing us a small kitchen knife each. He knocked on the wall, and down a chute came a ton of spuds that needed eyeing. 'And don't forget, take every eye out, and report to me when you have finished.' When we finished those, we rubbed our hands, pleased with what we had done, when bump, another load came down the chute. We were there all day, and I couldn't face potatoes for a while after that!

Initiative was not favoured, the whole idea being to instil total and unquestioning obedience so that the unit functioned as one. Any 'Jack the lads' were singled out and made to conform ... and sooner or later they did, the easy way or the hard way. Faced with all this, some tried to get discharged on medical grounds. The MOs knew all the scams, but that didn't stop them being tried:

- the bad back;
- deliberately worsening rashes caused by irritation of the uniform;
- swallowing cotton wool;
- wearing boots at night to deteriorate the condition of feet;
- feigning madness.

Pulling together

Competition was encouraged between the huts, often resulting in nocturnal sabotage. However, this had the desired effect of engendering camaraderie within each flight or platoon.

Case study – George Eckley

We each had to do guard duty every ten days or so, and for this six men were required from the various platoons. Seven men were actually selected, but the best turned-out man received a tap on the shoulder from the Duty Sergeant. The 'stickman', as he was termed, was not required, having earned the right to return to his billet. I was fortunate enough to be the stickman the first time I reported for guard duty – I was delighted, so were the rest of the platoon. However, this resulted in certain pressures. A second nomination as stickman brought with it release from all future guard duties during basic training, and the right to go into town. It also bestowed great honour on the platoon.

All hopes now rested on me, so no effort was spared when it came to my second guard duty. The lads treated me like royalty: a newer greatcoat was lent to me; my trousers were turned inside out and the creases sharpened with *Fairy* soap (it had to be *Fairy* as there was no perfume), and the hems were weighted to enhance the way they hung. I was also made to stand on a table whilst my boots were given the final polish, being lifted down bodily so that I didn't have to bend my foot and risk the boots being creased. No effort was spared, and the bull – and expectations – expended on my appearance had to be seen to be believed.

I had never been so nervous as during that second inspection, but the eventual tap on my shoulder was worth the wait. I think the whole camp must have known the outcome when I returned to the hut, because the celebrations were nothing if not loud.

Officer training

If you were 'encouraged' to apply for a short-term commission, or to sign on as a regular, you might like to describe the selection criteria and the aptitude tests for potential officer material. Record your reactions to the outcome – whatever the decision was – and the implications this had on your service career.

Postings

How you enjoyed the remainder of your time in National Service was largely dependent on where you served and in what capacity. For some it was an educational and enjoyable time seeing the world and experiencing other cultures. Others learnt a trade or pursued one started in civvy street. A third category might have found their time futile and tedious, whilst a fourth group may have feared for their lives. Describe your feelings on being told what you would be doing next and where you were going.

Case study – Ron Larkin

I was told that I would be working in the RAF Records Office, Gloucester, as a Machine Recording Operator and that I was going to attend a six-week training course. Everything seemed to be very civilised here; I wasn't being shouted at; I wasn't continually being called 'Airman' and people were explaining things in a constructive manner. So there was a different life in the RAF after Hednesford!

I was taken, with all my kit, to Hut 248 and given a bed and exactly the same type of wardrobe and cabinet as we had before. Whilst the hut was reasonably tidy, it wasn't bulled up to the standard to which I had become accustomed. This completely different and relaxed atmosphere was rather off-putting and somewhat of an anti-climax after the rarefied atmosphere of basic training camp.

I was told to report to Warrant Officer Monroe at the Admin Office the following morning at 0900 hrs. 'Nine o'clock,' I thought, 'this must be like a holiday camp compared with where I have just come from!'

Some national servicemen had dangerous overseas postings alongside war veterans like Robert Measures.

Case study – Robert Measures

Calcutta erupted in violent riots towards the end of 1945. The rioters had a particularly disgraceful habit of tying soldiers to the steering wheel of a vehicle and then setting it on fire. In slight mitigation, there were many military-type civilian-owned vehicles, painted in Army colour, being driven with the usual abandon around Calcutta and, when the inevitable accident occurred, the quickly gathering mob assumed that it had been caused by the unloved military. Recognising this, the Army decreed that the bonnets of all its transport should be painted with distinctive wide yellow 'tiger' stripes. Thankfully, this took most of the heat out of the situation.

The final analysis

It will be interesting to record how you felt at the end of your National Service as well as a longer-term reflection with the benefit of hindsight. It might be that you did not appreciate quite how much you had learned, something that only became apparent in later years. This could relate to skills you were taught, or perhaps more to do with your personal development, confidence and self-sufficiency.

Points to ponder

- Given your time again, would you want to do National Service?
- What was the value of National Service to the country?
- What did you feel about it ending in 1960?

Top tips

🖎   Speech can embellish a good story. Artistic licence is allowed where you cannot remember the actual words spoken, always ensuring that they are not libellous. When it comes to barrack room language, you might want to tone it down anyway!

🖎   Whilst not wanting to miss out on a good story, take care with the emphasis – if you write something that is purely malicious, it might say more about you than the person concerned!

Love and Marriage 10

Whilst initially following a conventional view of marriage, other situations are considered later in the chapter.

Meeting your partner

Some of the things to consider here include:

- where you met, and how you came to be there, especially if chance played a part;
- what your first impressions were;
- the first impressions of your partner about you;
- when you realised that this might be the one for you;

- any awkward, surprising, embarrassing or tender moments;
- whether you were looking for a partner, or perhaps were disillusioned with the opposite sex for one reason or another and actually didn't want a relationship ... or maybe you considered yourself 'on the shelf' at the grand old age of 25;
- any overriding desires to leave home, and if this meant getting married, here was your chance!

Women are particularly good at remembering all sorts of romantic details, the more that are included, the better. The wider family will be mesmerised by what you write, and even if they have heard some of the stories before, it is always better to have them recorded on paper for posterity.

Case study – Duncan Williams

It was at the Tobeys' Christmas party in 1947 that I first met Pam Mackenzie. I had known the Tobey family for years, and so had Pam, although strangely our paths had not crossed before. Various games had been planned for the evening, involving teams of two. Small novelties from crackers were placed in ashtrays, in the cloakroom for the men, and the bedrooms for the ladies. As we took our coats off we were told to select one of these novelties and then look for our partner. I selected a small silver horse and then found Pam with the corresponding novelty. I was very happy with this outcome. Incidentally, I still have the novelty horse ... and so does my wife, Pam.

Charles Durrett resorted to shock tactics.

Case study – Warrant Officer Charles Durrett

On my first day at the new base I went off to the Sergeants' Mess for lunch, sitting at an unoccupied table. A few minutes later, two ladies sat down, one at the end of the table, the other opposite. Having acknowledged their presence, we had no further conversation as it was nose-in-the-trough time. Shortly afterwards, we were joined by another lady who had an obvious physical disability in walking. Despite this, she was by no means unattractive and aroused my interest. She also sat opposite me and I acknowledged her presence. As the other two ladies were well known to her, a three-way conversation began. Most of it appeared to centre upon the previous evening's television programme on squirrels. Although I was not included in the conversation, it was nevertheless apparent to me that I was an object of interest, if only because I was a new face.

To eliminate any possible difficulties for the ladies to invite me into their conversation, I resorted to a well-tried tactic I have used many times and that is to make a remark which, if not in any way outrageous, at least is certainly unorthodox and will assuredly bring things to a halt for a while. I said, 'You can always tell a virgin by the way she holds her knife.' Immediately three pairs of eyes dropped to their left hand. Two wore wedding rings, the third did not and thus a sense of intrigue was created. I then told them who I was and I was considerably surprised when the unmarried lady, Jean, announced she had heard all about me from my days at No. 61 Group HQ at Kenley.

(Charles and Jean later married.)

Courting days

You may wish to write about your values and what behaviour was acceptable for courting couples. Opportunities for expressing your passion were also limited – few people had cars, and living with parents came with its own constraints.

Case study – Mary Robinson

In June Derek and I went on holiday together to a guesthouse in Filey. Of course, Derek and I had to have separate bedrooms – on different floors – and the proprietors kept an eye on us to make sure we were not left alone indoors!

The proposal

What you remember of the proposal will be read eagerly. From the man's point of view, you might remember:

- if you were nervous;
- if you had any doubts that she might turn you down;
- if you knew that she would accept ... after all, she'd been badgering you for months!;
- your planning of the proposal, perhaps having bought the ring and even involved others in your arrangements for the special moment;
- if you had been to see her father to ask his permission in advance;
- if she proposed to you!

From the lady's point of view, you might remember:

    ❧ if you were caught by surprise, or perhaps you knew the proposal was coming;

    ❧ if you were worried that he might never propose;

    ❧ seeing how ill at ease he felt, and fearing that he was going to end the relationship;

    ❧ what your reaction was;

    ❧ whether you actually proposed to him … because someone had to make a decision;

    ❧ any details about the occasion, what you were wearing, where you were, the weather, etc. – after all, you are far more likely to remember such details than your husband!

Feelings, reactions and the actual words spoken all add to the story.

Case study – Leonard Hall

At the age of 13, I appeared in a school play called *The Jeffersons*, produced, as always, by Billy Minns. I took the part of Rosie Jefferson, an attractive (at least, I hope I was) 21-year-old north-country girl. In the script, Rosie received a proposal of marriage. The producer, realising my inexperience in these matters, instructed me as to how a modest young lady receiving such a proposal would react – averting her eyes, blushing and being generally embarrassed. Little did he know that I would put his coaching to good use when, 15 years later, I proposed to his daughter. I do not think she achieved all three of these responses, but suffice it to say that Betty and I have been happily married for 54 years so far. Had Betty's father lived to see us together, I am sure he would have approved!

How the parents were asked or informed, and their reactions should also be included.

Case study – Jean Dudley

Peter's proposal of marriage to me was far from romantic. He was about to lose his home, I had moved into my own furnished accommodation in an old Victorian house in Croydon, and he said that it would be beneficial tax-wise to get married – forever the accountant! I remember going to see Mum and Dad, and when we told them the date of our intended wedding on 31 October 1953, Dad looked at the calendar and said, 'Good God, that's in ten days' time!'

Parental concerns

Your parents may have considered that you were too young to get married, or perhaps they were concerned about the suitability of the match or a large age difference. It will be interesting to record how such obstacles were overcome and how valid their concerns proved to be.

Planning the wedding

Consider such things as:

- ⚘ how much time you had to arrange the wedding;
- ⚘ the reason for selecting that date – for example, midweek to fit in with half-day closing;
- ⚘ what sort of wedding you wanted, and how much of it became a reality;
- ⚘ who was paying for what, and any problems this caused;
- ⚘ your bridesmaids, best man, etc.;
- ⚘ what you both wore and any problems in acquiring the outfits;
- ⚘ any difficulties in booking the church, reception ...;
- ⚘ what music was chosen and why;

⚘ whether rationing had any impact on the wedding;

⚘ hen or stag celebrations, especially if any interesting stories are involved;

⚘ any doubts creeping in and how they were addressed.

Case study – Ann Davies

Everything went according to plan apart from when I decided on a special perm for the big day. I wanted to save some money and made the mistake of doing this myself. Having never done this before, the end result was a total disaster and I had to go to the hairdresser's in Winchester to see what they could do; there was no way I could get married with my hair in such a frizzy mess.

Apparently it was beyond redemption and they had no alternative other than to chop it off. I had never been into this hairdresser's before and they seemed to operate a strange system. After my hair had been cut (very short), it was then set in rollers. When the hairdresser came to comb it out I had to sit in another chair and face the boss so that she could watch every move the hairdresser made, presumably to ensure everything was done correctly. With the little bit of hair I had left, there was not much she could have done wrong! I certainly found it embarrassing sitting in front of this lady for what seemed an eternity.

Keith did not see my short hair until after the wedding service because of the veil. I often wonder, if he had seen it before, would he have changed his mind!

Your wedding day

Weddings did not tend to be the extravaganzas so common today. It was usual to have a modest afternoon reception, often back at the parents' house, before the bride and groom slipped off on honeymoon (if they had one) in the late afternoon or early evening. For others it might have been a morning registry office wedding, followed by a few drinks in the pub. When it comes to the actual day itself, there is plenty more to consider:

- any last-minute nerves and how they were overcome;
- who conducted the service, especially if you knew the vicar well or there was any family connection;
- who attended, and, if travelling long distances, where they stayed;
- any disasters with dress, bridesmaids, flowers, car, photographer, reception, ring, etc.;
- concerns about the weather and what it turned out like;
- any amusing, worrying, horrifying incidents during the service;
- your feelings during the wedding;
- anything you remember about the speeches;
- your overall impressions of how the day went.

Colours, fabrics, flower scents, feelings and emotions all make for excellent reading, although women tend to be better at remembering such details.

Case study – Lil Fulker

I shook all the way through the ceremony, tears trickling down my face. I did have a handkerchief, but as it was part of the traditional 'something old, something new, something borrowed, something blue' and was therefore tucked away in my shoe, rather than sniff my way through the ceremony I borrowed Les's hanky from the top pocket of his suit!

Les did not even get around to buying his suit until the day before the wedding, which meant that he was not able to get an 'off the peg' suit that fitted. The trousers were so loose around the waist that, in the absence of a belt, he had to prevent them from falling down by tying a tie around his waist! That tale gives a good indication of his laid-back character.

The reception

For most couples, the reception was a modest affair, but some were fortunate enough to pull out all the stops.

Case study – Don Coombe

We had what was quite a grand affair for 1948 – a sit-down reception for 45 people. The church hall, where the reception was held, banned intoxicating liquor. This was a blessing so far as I was concerned, although a friend of Dad's provided a bottle of Champagne to toast the bride and groom. This was my first taste of bubbly – I still prefer lager.

The wedding breakfast, a sit down three-course meal, cost the grand sum of five shillings (25p) per head. My buttonhole at half a crown (12½p) was expensive, but Betty's 9ct gold wedding ring at £1.11s (£1.55) was not.

I borrowed £50 from my boss to cover the expenses of the day and anticipated paying it back over a period of months. My salary then was £200 per year.

Our wedding day coincided with Derby Day. Although not a gambling man, on looking down the list of runners 'My Love' focused my attention. Yes – it won! I had backed it with a great deal of faith – one pound each way. At a starting price of 66–1, I was able to pay for the reception and our honeymoon.

As you probably only received a few wedding presents, you might be able to remember some of them and who they were from. Are any still in use today?

Wartime weddings

By necessity, these tended to be frugal and functional.

Case study – Joan Hassall

Beryl offered to lend me her white satin wedding dress with a short train, but I declined her kind offer because it would have meant the expense of bridesmaids' dresses, flowers and a more formal reception – things we couldn't afford. I decided to get married in a suit as it was much more practical and useful afterwards. I found a light blue Harris tweed suit at *Dingles*, and a pale pink blouse to wear with it. I wasn't much into wearing a hat, and anyway they were in short supply and quite expensive, so I made my own headdress from pale blue and pink feathers attached to a small felt base.

Dad had managed to find a bottle of whisky from some source – still in short supply – and the cook on Steve's ship promised to make a wedding cake. We also managed to book a photographer, but the number of photos was restricted because of the shortage of film.

When we had gone to buy the wedding ring, again we had had little choice. We could choose either a 9ct 'utility' ring, or a 22ct more decorative ring which was way beyond what we could afford. So it was the plain, solid ring that we had, but it has lasted, as did our marriage.

We returned home after the ceremony for the afternoon, but in the evening we went to Gran's and had a family party. Later we left and went with Aunt Beat, Uncle Frank and Franky to their home in Totnes, where we spent a few days on honeymoon.

If you got married in the war, describe some of the sacrifices that had to be made:

- a cardboard wedding cake, with a drawer in it for a real piece of cake for the wedding couple;
- a maximum of six photographs;
- no church bells ringing out;
- friends and relatives in the Forces not being able to attend the wedding.

The honeymoon

Due to the expense, or having to be back at work, perhaps a honeymoon passed you by. If you promised yourself one at a later date, inform the reader whether this ever materialised. Even for those fortunate enough to have a honeymoon, it may have been a case of a weekend away, perhaps staying with relatives … and it was not unknown for some couples to be accompanied by other members of the family. If you had a honeymoon, there is likely to be a story or two attached.

Case study – Mary Robinson

The arrangements were for George to drive us to Doncaster to catch the 6.15 pm train to London, but when we arrived there was no train! Derek's friend who had looked up the times had made a mistake and the next train was not until 10.15 pm. Derek, George, Betty and I went to the pictures to kill the time and saw *The Love Lottery*. We sat in the front row of the circle, and as it was quite warm I opened my coat and took my scarf off. Confetti came flying out and drifted over the edge of the circle and down into the stalls below. I daredn't look over!

We reached Kings Cross at about 1.00 am and took a taxi to our hotel, but as we were so late they put us up in a small attic room so as not to disturb other guests. There were no en suite rooms in most hotels in those days. I undressed on a piece of paper so that the remaining confetti would not be scattered (a tip I had been given by a friend). Next morning, after breakfast, we were offered a larger room and a member of staff showed us the way. When she opened the door there was confetti everywhere. She exclaimed, 'Oh, these newlyweds; don't they make a mess?' I agreed with her, and we went to fetch our cases. I folded up the newspaper with the confetti in, took it to the new room and then emptied it onto the floor with the other confetti. Derek just laughed, but we were saved the embarrassment of being caught out as newlyweds!

Giving up work

For many women, getting married meant losing their job. If this was your experience, it needs to be recorded.

Case study – Sylvia Culverhouse

I had to leave my job at the *Co-op* when I got married, because married women weren't allowed to be Chief Clerk. However, my second in command suddenly had a nervous breakdown and the third clerk was not yet qualified, so a special concession was made ... I was allowed to remain on in the post for a few months to train up the third clerk to take over my position, at which point I was out of a job!

Finding love in later life

If you have been married more than once, how much you choose to include about each of your weddings, and in what detail, is a choice only you can make. Where children are involved, either your own and/or any inherited from your new spouse, consideration will need to be given to their thoughts and feelings.

Case study – Joan Belk

One day when I popped in to see my brother at work he introduced me to a friend of his called Albert. We started chatting, and continued even when Ernest was called away. Albert took me to the bus stop and then asked if I would like to go to the cinema to see *El Cid*, so we made a date for the next day. When I arrived home I just couldn't believe what I had done. Going out with a man, well it wasn't like me was it? Anyway, there was something about him that I liked – I think fate smiled on me that day. When Mum came home, I told her about Albert and she was highly delighted – she thought I was getting a right old maid and that I was going to be a man-hater for the rest of my life.

Albert and I found that we had a lot in common and shared the same sense of humour. It was lovely to talk to somebody who understood what I was on about. My first husband only knew four subjects – money, sport, drinking and womanising, so I had always been limited in what I could talk to him about. Anything deeper than these and he was stymied.

Albert and I started to see each other regularly, and one night after the pictures he asked if I would be his girl. I told him that I thought I was, to which he replied, 'Oh, did you – that's lovely.' Six weeks after we met, Albert proposed to me and I was delighted to accept.

The single life

At a time when marriage was seen as the norm, women especially could be made to feel uncomfortable about remaining single. Phrases such as 'being on the shelf', and 'not having met Mr Right', from well-meaning friends and family, only made matters worse.

What you share with your readers has nothing to do with any relationship status. Few married people reveal their innermost thoughts or justify their decisions, and others should not feel compelled to do so either. The telling of your story should come naturally, so whether you chose to remain single, got married, or were dictated to by events, just let your writing flow.

Divorce and difficult marriages

Writing about divorce or an unhappy marriage needs to be handled sensitively, especially where children are involved. If feelings are still raw it might be best to wait a while before committing anything to paper. Alternatively, you can say that things did not work out, or were not easy, and that it is still too painful to write about.

Words can be used both diplomatically and ambiguously, and sometimes more can be said by writing very little. Also, just because you write something does not mean that it has to appear in your book, but the very process of writing can be helpful. As regards a child's divorce, it is worth checking that what you have written is acceptable, prior to producing your book.

Death of loved ones

Writing about the death of a partner or loved one can be therapeutic and help with the grieving process, although a period of time may need to pass before you feel able to do this. In addition to providing the opportunity to record your own tribute, and possibly also a review of their life, it can be comforting to know that their memory will live on through your book. An obituary can be printed in your book, or the funeral service card inserted into a wallet attached to the inside back cover.

Points to ponder

- What was the most romantic time of your life?
- When did you feel most contented?
- What is the nicest compliment you have been given?

Top tips

- If appropriate, ask your partner to write about their early life to complement your book, especially if it is for the family. They may also be happy to write about a special occasion, like your first meeting or, perhaps, your wedding day. In such cases, try not to confer ... as it is fascinating to read who has remembered what!

- If writing about a special person in your life who is no longer around, consider including a favourite photograph of them as a respectful conclusion to that part of the book.

The Middle Years 11

In looking at the middle years of life, this chapter considers such topics as leaving home, buying a house, settling down and having a family. The decades following Britain's post-war gloom also saw great changes in lifestyle, opportunity and expectation, and so whatever your domestic circumstances, the broad expanse of this chapter is sure to open up a host of memories.

Taking lodgings

With accommodation being hard to come by in post-war Britain, it may have been a case of moving in with family or in-laws, with all the trials and tribulations that this brought:

- ✎ record who else was in the house, their ages and their various comings and goings;
- ✎ describe the bathroom arrangements and what privacy, if any, this offered;

    ☞ explain what part of the house you had and if it was considered rude to keep to yourselves;

    ☞ if younger siblings were about, include an anecdote or two about how awkward they could be;

    ☞ the cooking and eating arrangements are likely to have been fraught with two women sharing a kitchen ... particularly in-laws;

    ☞ you might even want to record how living with family in a small house and creaky floorboards affected your love life!;

    ☞ describe your efforts to find somewhere else to live, and if this caused any friction within the family, or indeed if your spouse was quite content to continue with the arrangement.

At least the Fulkers were lucky enough to find their own accommodation.

Case study – Lil Fulker

Our room was 6ft by 8ft and too small to accommodate a double bed, so we had a three-foot bed which we positioned lengthways against the wall. A two-foot square homemade wardrobe was between the bed and the window, to the left of which was a small set of drawers and a chair – when Lesley came along we placed her cot in between these, effectively blocking off the fireplace. We hung a small blanket on the side of the cot to stem any draughts. The room was totally full with the exception of an 18-inch path between the door and the window, and our sole possessions were contained within that tiny space. We owned one small suitcase, and the rest of our belongings were housed in cardboard boxes stacked on top of the wardrobe and underneath the bed.

Next to our bedroom was a toilet, but no wash basin. A few steps up from the toilet was a small kitchen which we shared with another couple and an old lady. The sink was barely 18 inches square ... I have never seen a smaller one. The ancient cooker had four burners, but only two of them worked, and an extremely temperamental thermostat supposedly controlled the oven temperature. There was also an open fire grate.

We had no money for fuel, so we gathered sticks on Sheen Common and the landlady let me clean her bedroom once a week in return for a bucket of coal. One bucket was just enough to light the fire each evening, but not to replenish it, so when it died down we went to bed with a hot water bottle and sat under the eiderdown listening to a speaker which ran from the landlady's wireless downstairs.

A home of your own

Corporation or council houses were in great demand, but rather than climbing the list, many couples found themselves going down it. To provide more housing, prefabs started springing up, but for most it was a case of having to be imaginative in finding accommodation.

Case study – Alf Sore

Our firm was doing some minor conversions on Warmingford Aerodrome, converting Nissen huts which had been used by the American Air Force. This was only very minor work, like making them watertight (… well, almost!) and installing coke-burning stoves. While I was working there one of the huts became empty, so Kath and I jumped at the chance to move in and become squatters. People were often moving in and out of these huts, using them as temporary accommodation on a first-come first-served basis.

It was very disheartening to arrive on a cold December day with a three-month old baby and look into an almost empty RAF hut. We had gathered some furniture together, which amounted to a second-hand bedroom suite, a table, a couple of chairs, a few odds and ends and, most important of all, a baby's cot.

We soon got cracking, and once the fire was lit and we had all had a meal, things didn't look so bad. But then we had a terrible shock … I pressed the light switch and nothing happened – terrific, no electricity. I had a quick look round and discovered that ours was the only hut without a light. So it was bed by candlelight … at least it was romantic.

Buying your first house

Home ownership became more popular after the war with greater availability of mortgages. Even then, properties were not easy to come by.

Case study – Joan Hassall

As Steve was now eligible for a mortgage we started house-hunting. There was very little property on the market at the time and the agents could only offer us one or two. We had also been buying the local paper, but again properties for sale were absent. *The Evening Herald* was printed in the city centre, so we went there and waited to buy a newspaper 'straight off the press'. There was just one advert, a house for sale at Elburton on the outskirts of Plymouth. There was no phone number but the address was given, so we were in the car and away, hoping to be the first applicants.

An elderly man opened the door and was amazed that his advert had appeared and got a response so quickly. The property was a two-bedroom semi-detached bungalow, with a garden at the front and an even larger one at the rear. Mr Bowden, the owner, was obviously a keen gardener, with flowers and vegetables in abundance.

We liked the bungalow; it was in a good state of repair and decoration, and the price was fair. We agreed to buy it and went straight to our solicitors. The following week we visited the bungalow again and Mr Bowden told us that he had been inundated with callers. One woman persisted in trying to make him sell it to her by leaving a blank cheque, so he could name his own price, but Mr Bowden refused all other offers. As he told us later, he had given his word, had shaken hands on it and he would not go back on it. He was one of life's true gentlemen.

Making your house into a home

Furnishing your first home is likely to have been an exciting time, associated with memories of having to beg, steal or borrow whatever you could … maybe even improvising with orange boxes and tea chests for a while. You may have received some useful wedding presents, and perhaps you can remember saving hard for other special items. Some of this furniture will be easy to recall, especially if it is still in use today.

Aspirations of luxury

Whilst you may not have had many of the following luxuries initially, they are sure to have made an impact when they did arrive. Perhaps you remember seeing some of them first at the Ideal Home Exhibition and dreaming of the time when you could afford them:

- a vacuum cleaner, preferably a *Hoover*;
- a refrigerator and its own ice box;
- a washing machine, perhaps with an electric mangle attachment;
- a twin-tub or separate spin-dryer;
- a *Flatley* clothes drier;
- a steam iron;

- a television set;
- fitted carpets.

Do-it-yourself

Drab post-war Britain gave way to the optimism of the 1950s and 1960s, with fashion, style and colour abounding. Homes were similarly being transformed, and for those wanting to have a go themselves, Barry Bucknell was on hand to offer advice. In writing about your early attempts at decorating you might remember:

- scraping for hours to remove generations of wallpaper;
- wallpaper with the maker's name along the side and having to trim each length to get a straight edge (some shops offered a trimming service at one shilling a roll);
- a little later, wallpaper being scored along the length so that a sharp tap would remove the edge ... well, that was the theory;
- mixing flour and water as an adhesive to hang the paper;
- borders printed on a roll of wallpaper having to be cut into strips along the length;
- having to stir the spirit-based paint for ages before it was ready for use.

Those in rented accommodation had little incentive to improve where they lived, even if it was allowed by the landlord. However, as more people started to own their own homes, so the DIY industry developed. Disasters are particularly worth recording, as are any larger projects, particularly if enthusiasm waned before they were completed! Projects might include:

- covering panelled doors with hardboard;
- building shelves, units and wardrobes;
- knocking down internal walls;
- opening up the stairs;
- building a serving hatch;
- putting up coving, picture rails or dado rails;
- enclosing a fireplace once central heating had been installed.

Of course, there might also be larger projects like an extension or building a garage. If you still live in the house, wander around to see how it has changed over the years.

Gardening

The garden should not be overlooked during this review. If you and/or your spouse have green fingers, it will be natural to write about the pleasure derived from gardening and how your interest, and the garden, evolved over the years. There may also be the occasional DIY project associated with the garden, like erecting a greenhouse, laying a patio, or digging a pond.

Having children

As children grow, it is sometimes easy to forget the amazing joy of their birth:

- the overwhelming feelings of love;
- the wonderment of the miracle of birth;
- the incredible complexity of their tiny bodies;
- the fear of not being good enough parents;
- the concern over their well-being and safety;
- the difficulty of choosing names;
- the aspirations you have for them.

Recording your feelings of the time will make for great reading, especially for the children who are being written about. You may still be able to remember your thoughts on discovering that you were going to be a parent in the first place and any plans and worries you had during the pregnancy. Then there was the birth itself – the pain, exhaustion and emotion of the mother, and the detached lack of involvement for the father … he was very unlikely to have been present at the birth. You might want to record:

ॐ   any amusing stories relating to their birth;

ॐ   why you chose the names you did;

ॐ   who the godparents were and why;

ॐ   each child's first words and funny expressions;

ॐ   any amusing incidents and mannerisms;

ॐ   any involvement of the wider family in bringing up your child;

ॐ   the development of their character;

ॐ   whether you followed 'expert' advice from the likes of Dr Spock.

Children growing up

Writing about children growing up is similar to writing about your own childhood, but from their perspective. You might therefore like to review the early chapters of this book from your children's viewpoint. In the process, interesting comparisons may emerge regarding discipline, character traits, talents, etc., as well as a growing empathy with your own parents.

Writing about children

When writing about children, the general rule is to concentrate on the years until they leave home, with the caveat of diplomacy. Amusing incidents of them growing up and their characters developing will make for fascinating reading, as will their achievements and various milestones like schooldays, hobbies, memorable birthdays and holidays. They will also expect to read about those incidents that have already passed into family folklore, and as long as you poke fun at yourself, it should be accepted by the family that they are treated in the same way.

If there is anything about which you feel uncomfortable, consider omitting it or else discussing it in advance so that there are no awkward surprises when the book is produced. This may relate to delicate health issues or matters of the heart; for example, writing about their old flames might not be appropriate.

After the children have left home, the usual practice is to write about any major areas like marriage, children, career progression, house moves, etc. If they want to write more, that is up to them, but this book is about you and your life.

Learning to drive

Whilst some learned to drive in the war or during their National Service, for most people it was a case of waiting until the need or opportunity arose. With car ownership becoming increasingly affordable during the 1950s and 1960s more people learned to drive, but even then relatively few drivers were women. You might remember such details as:

- how old you were when you learned to drive;
- who taught you and in what car;
- if you had formal lessons, and how much they cost;
- if it was a friend or member of the family, how harmonious the lessons were!;
- how many tests you took before you passed, and any mishaps;
- what it felt like to drive by yourself for the first time.

Whilst you will probably not want to list all the cars you have owned over the years, there may be one or two favourites … you might even recall the registration numbers or perhaps the names you had for them! Any accidents, interesting incidents or brushes with the law are usually worth a mention, as are early experiences of driving when cars were less sophisticated.

Case study – Joy Kennedy

On Sundays we usually went out in Angus's car. This was an old dark green 1938 *Morris 8*, two-door, top speed 45mph, which you had to double de-clutch when you changed gear. I was never allowed to drive his car, this being the reason given. Whenever we came to a big hill, we had to wait at the bottom until there was nothing in front of us, so that we could have a clear run, without stopping, to the top. This was the only way we could get up.

Holidays

Other people's holiday snaps can become tedious if viewed in quantity, and the same will be true if your reader is subjected to a detailed account of all your holidays over the years. The answer is to select a few special ones, perhaps those relating to early years with the children, or those which are particularly notable for one reason or another, like camping, *Butlin's*, going abroad for the first time and early experiences of package holidays. Again, amusing anecdotes will entertain the reader, as will tortuous journeys and nightmare holidays. A look through your photograph albums may well provide plenty of material.

Special events

Whilst looking at the photo album, you might be reminded of some special family days that jog a memory or two:

- christenings;
- birthdays;
- Christmas;
- school plays and concerts;
- bonfire night.

National events might also feature in your photo album, like attending the Festival of Britain in 1951 and seeing the Dome of Discovery, Skylon and the Guinness Clock.

Whilst the history notes section can also be referred to, a few special events merit particular attention:

- the Coronation of Queen Elizabeth II on 2 June 1953;
- Roger Bannister breaking the four-minute mile on 6 May 1954;
- the assassination of President Kennedy on 22 November 1963;
- the death, and state funeral of Winston Churchill in late January 1965;
- England winning the World Cup on 30 July 1966;
- the assassination of Martin Luther King Jr on 9 April 1968;
- The investiture of the Prince of Wales at Caernarvon Castle on 1 July 1969;
- Man setting foot on the moon on 21 July 1969;
- decimalisation being introduced to Britain on 15 February 1971;
- Princess Anne's marriage to Captain Mark Phillips on 14 November 1973;
- The Queen's Silver Jubilee on 2 June 1977.

You've never had it so good

With changes in society, technology, music, fashion and food, your lifestyle during these middle years is likely to have been significantly different from that experienced by your parents at a similar age.

Society

Whilst most women stayed at home to look after children, many returned to work once their little darlings started school. Mass-produced labour-saving devices and electrical appliances made it easier to run a home … even if they were bought on hire–purchase. Central heating was a further boon, removing the need for dirty, time-consuming fires.

Television

Televisions gained greater acceptance with the Coronation of Queen Elizabeth II in 1953, but even then they were a luxury enjoyed by very few. You might remember the minuscule size of the sets, often requiring a magnification device for better vision, the long time it took to warm up … and the dot in the middle of the screen when you turned it off. Then there was the test card, the poor and infrequent reception, and it was all in black and white, of course.

Case study – Ken Baxter

Getting a television was a great occasion, and even though the programmes were very limited and only transmitted for a few hours, it was all very exciting. Children's programmes were on for an hour or so, then transmission closed down for a couple of hours before the evening broadcasts started. Even these did not go on too long, with the station closing down for the night at about 10.30. Audiences were also treated with the greatest respect and all the presenters were dressed in formal evening-wear, which for the men obviously included a bow tie.

There was a slot meter attached to the rented set and we had to insert a sixpence (2½p) for an hour's viewing. Every so often the man came round to empty the meter. The rental was less than the 6d per hour and so there was always a residual balance for us – in effect it formed quite a good way of saving … the more you watched the more you saved!

You might like to write about some of your favourite programmes and how the television changed life in your home.

Even with the advent of television, the radio still held a place in the nation's heart, as audiences for The Goons and Tony Hancock proved. You might have even been able to pick up a pirate radio station to indulge your love of pop music.

Music and fashion

With hindsight it is easy to form opinions of the major influences of the 1950s, 1960s and 1970s, but it will be interesting to read what it was like to live through these years and how they affected you and your family – the excitement or horror that you felt with the onset of each new craze, be they Teddy Boys, Beatniks, Mods and Rockers or Hippies. The radical changes in music and fashion and the rise of the 'teenager' were tied in with the introduction of the pill, leading to a sexual revolution as well as a change in lifestyle and attitudes. Reference to the music sections of the history notes at the back of the book will help jog further memories.

'Modern' materials

If your life was transformed by such materials as Bakelite, Formica, Plastic, Pyrex, Polyester, Crimplene, Courtelle, Flocked Nylon, Winceyette, Dacron or some other wonder product, you might want to mention them in your book.

Food

Fridges, freezers, pre-prepared food and, later, microwaves, revolutionised the way people cooked. Menus also changed, particularly with the influence of Indian, Italian and Chinese dishes. You might be able to recall when you first tried some of these cuisines and what you thought about them. Restaurants became popular for an evening out, or perhaps you had dinner parties at home.

Social life

In addition to food-related activities, you might also recall such initiatives as beetle drives, bridge, treasure hunts, games evenings and other organised events. If you were involved with any clubs, societies, the church, children's schools or with your own group of friends, these can also be included.

Making ends meet

As most mothers usually stayed at home to look after the children, any additional income was probably welcome. This may have involved:

- joining a Christmas club to save regularly;
- collecting *Green Shield* stamps;
- hire purchase agreements;
- joining a catalogue or perhaps even running one yourself;
- getting a part-time job;
- working from home – maybe childcare, taking in ironing, or being paid a pittance on piece-work.

Points to ponder

- What are your feelings concerning these years?
- How did your lifestyle change?
- What organisations did you become involved with?
- What new hobbies did you take up?
- How did you like to spend your spare time?
- What was your ideal holiday?

Top tips

- In thinking about friends, it might help to look at your Christmas card list and old address books to refresh your memory – after all, if you have been sending Christmas cards to someone for 30+ years, surely they deserve a mention in your book!

- Don't worry if you find that you have less to write about the later years. Unless you have had a stunning or diverse career, or a particularly dynamic later life, this will often be the case. The earlier years are likely to be more detailed, simply because so much has changed since then.

Working Life

12

Those who have had a distinguished or diverse career may write several chapters, whilst for others work may be a relatively minor part of the book. Indeed, some may have covered the period relating to their working lives already, especially women who gave up work when they got married and never sought employment again.

Due to the vast diversity of working lives, you might like to review this chapter to select those facets applicable to your story. If you have a significant amount to write, you can either cover everything in successive chapters or intersperse it between the other areas of your life.

The principles discussed in Chapter 6 – Early Working Life, will be worth reviewing alongside some of the more in-depth material covered here.

General guidelines

In writing about your work, it must be remembered that not all readers will be as well informed about the industry in which you worked. You might therefore need to provide some background information and avoid, or at least explain, any jargon. It is also recommended that you include a few anecdotes that illustrate your work. These can be reasonably in-depth if they are accessible to a lay audience.

If there is a heavily technical project you want to write about, or perhaps a report you would like to include, consider inserting it as an appendix and providing a reference at the appropriate point in your writing. This prevents an imbalance in your book, whilst still incorporating information that you consider important and which will be appreciated by some of your audience.

Essentially, work anecdotes should be treated in the same way as any good raconteur would tell a story to an audience of mixed backgrounds – giving sufficient detail to create interest, whilst taking care not to bore. Balance is the key.

Setting the scene

If the war, National Service or further education led to a career change from your early working life, it will be helpful to explain your thought process or the sequence of events. Alternatively, you may have continued in the same industry, or even in the same company as your first job of work, and so can now elaborate on it. You might like to include more anecdotes and write about the characters and projects that became part of your working life. What were your feelings, and was this a job you could see yourself doing for the rest of your working life? If not, what did you do about it, or, if you stayed, how did you adjust your expectations?

Looking too young

If you felt that your age was a handicap in your early working life, were there any steps you adopted to look older, such as wearing make-up or growing a beard, carrying a briefcase or choosing more grown-up clothes?

Case study – Dr Bill Barton

When I qualified at the age of 22 I looked like a lad of 17, so I always wore a hat. Not only was it the fashion, it was the required dress for the profession. Dr Lamont always wore his 'Anthony Eden'; for me it was a 'pork-pie' trilby style. I always kept my hat on till they answered the door and I was across the threshold, for in the early days when the door opened they would gape and ask, 'Yes?'

'I'm the doctor.'

'The doctor? Yer too young to be a doctor. I was expecting Dr Lamont!'… and the door would shut. Once I was inside the house and had taken off my hat they found it impolite to throw me out.

Politics

Corporate and social politics are invariably a feature of the workplace. Whether you relished this or avoided it, an anecdote or two will make for interesting reading.

If your industry was unionised, how did this affect you and the work of the company, and how was it looked upon if you were an active member? Any stories relating to dangerous working conditions and accidents can be included here, along with such issues as equal pay, discrimination, time-keeping, smoking at work and overtime, etc.

Training and further study

If you sat exams or undertook further training you might like to include:

- who instigated it, and who paid for it;
- what was expected of you and how you met those demands;
- if you were expected to study outside of work hours, and what this amounted to;
- whether residential courses were provided;
- how your progress was assessed and if this involved re-sits;
- whether you relished the challenge or perhaps became disillusioned with your chosen career.

Writing about colleagues

You will probably want to write about some of your bosses and work colleagues, particularly the more charismatic and inspiring ones. If there is someone who took you under their wing and gave you a chance, this is your opportunity to thank them for believing in you. Similarly, if you met any famous people in the course of your work, you will want to write about them.

Being careful about libel

If writing negatively, care needs to be exercised to avoid being libellous – writing that will damage a person's reputation or livelihood. The law of libel relates only to living people. Even if what you write is true, you must have the evidence to prove it, and any court proceedings will be both traumatic and expensive. Even changing the name of a person is insufficient if they can be reasonably identified by what you write.

Climbing the corporate ladder

Whether you remained in the same company, or moved about to advance your career, you might like to write about the challenges and rewards of climbing the corporate ladder:

- how you adapted to positions of responsibility;
- what interesting projects you were involved with;
- if you were able to leave your work behind, or whether you worried excessively in the evenings and at weekends;
- how you dealt with personnel issues and how you feel you were regarded as a boss;
- what your skills and weaknesses were;
- how ambitious you were;
- how much travelling was involved and whether you had a company car;
- opportunities for overseas travel and whether your spouse could go with you;
- the social side of work, what was expected and whether it was a joy or a chore;
- the opportunity of a secondment – perhaps overseas;
- being relocated by your company, or perhaps moving house to get a new job, and all the hassles involved;
- being offered a sabbatical.

The changing face of industry

It is likely that your industry, along with most others, will have altered significantly during your career. The latter half of the twentieth century saw many major changes, mention of which will be relevant where they affected you:

- overseas competition;
- the decline in traditional industries and the emergence of new ones;

- new wonder materials like plastics, revolutionising some industries and killing off others;
- the march of new technology and sophisticated machinery on production lines;
- immigration;
- militant trade unions and their subsequent demise;
- computerisation with all the upheaval and changes it involved;
- modern communications – satellites, mobile phones, etc.;
- industries being relocated abroad.

The low points

Dealing with disappointment and difficult times alongside the successes makes for a balanced story. This could relate to accidents or illness, perhaps resulting in hospitalisation, surgery and a change of lifestyle. Redundancy, a long period off work, having to retrain, a career being cut short or bereavement will have major repercussions, giving you the opportunity of writing about how you coped, both at the time and in the longer term.

The high points

The happier times are far easier to write about.

Case study – Jean Dudley

In November 1947 Princess Elizabeth married Prince Philip and wedding presents poured in from all over the world. As Dad's company already supplied kitchen equipment to Buckingham Palace, it was decided to give a *Turmix*, a revolutionary new blender and liquidizer, as a wedding present. Monsieur Ronald Aubrey, the royal chef, required a demonstration and as I was already doing this at the Hotel and Catering Exhibition at Olympia, I was asked to go along to the Palace with Dad.

What a thrill! Dad's car was known and we were waved straight through the side gates and, after parking, into the huge kitchens accompanied by the King's Comptroller of Supplies. Soon I was showing Monsieur Aubrey and his staff the wonders of this new machine. I remember making a sandwich spread, which I was told would be used for the Queen's tea – that was Queen Elizabeth, the wife of King George VI.

Running your own business

Anyone who ran his or her own business will not be short of material. In addition to all of the above, there will be the excitement, red tape, personnel issues and pressures associated with any company. Your life story will, in effect, also be a history of the company, so consideration will have to be given to the various milestones, key workers, the winning of important contracts and changes in location.

Whilst people may look enviously at a thriving company, it is also useful to record that things were not always thus.

Case study – Helmut Rothenberg

A rent of £22 10s per quarter was very cheap, even then. However, this sum was not always easy to come by when I was setting out on my own in business. On one occasion I found myself unable to find the money for the rent and had to resort to selling my precious portable typewriter. I used this when I was working from home in the evening, but I had to raise the money somehow. I sold the typewriter for £25. One of the first presents that Annema bought me when she started working as a clerk at *The Times Book Club* in Marylebone was a replacement typewriter.

Points to ponder

- Which jobs did you most enjoy, and why?
- What was the proudest moment of your working life?
- Why did you choose the career you pursued?
- Who were the most important people in your working life?

Top tips

- Any articles about your work, possibly in a company magazine can also be included in your book. If it is a lengthy article, consider including it as an appendix to avoid creating an imbalance in the body of the text.

- Once word gets around that you have written a book, you will be surprised by the number of friends that ask to read it. If a friend of yours wrote a book, you would be delighted to get a mention – the same will be true of them. Something simple will suffice: 'We never see them enough, but we always love catching up with the Shaws and Molters whenever we can.' A catchall phrase will cover even more: 'The summer would not be the same without all our friends at Cippenham Bowls Club.'

The Later Years 13

This chapter will bring your story up to the present day. In addition to looking at such areas as children leaving home, retirement, new projects and grandchildren, consideration will also be given to how you might conclude your book.

Children leaving home

If you have children it will be interesting to record how you felt when each of them left home, especially the last or the only one. You may have been delighted, thinking that you would never get rid of them, but perhaps there was also a feeling of emptiness and 'what now'? How you dealt with this time and what difference it made to your life will make for fascinating reading.

Marriage of children

Diplomacy needs to be exercised when writing about children and their partners. If there are potentially sensitive areas, it might be worth seeking clearance before anything is committed to the book. Then there are the emotions and practicalities of letting go of your precious offspring. This may have involved a sense of déjà vu.

Case study – Lil Fulker

In August, Michael and Lesley announced that they wanted to get married! We put forward the following arguments: they had not known each other long enough; they were, at 18 and 20, too young; they had no money; and they had nowhere to live.

Their answers were simply:

'You two had only known each other for three months when you decided to get married';

'You were 18 and 21 plus two weeks when you got married';

'Dad owed £2 and Mum had nine pence'; and

'You had nowhere to live. We will live in a tent in a field as long as we can be together.'

Family celebrations

Special family occasions are worth considering: weddings, notable anniversaries (silver, pearl, ruby, etc.), christenings, retirement and significant birthdays for close members of the family (21st, 30th, 40th, etc.).

The next generation

Becoming a grandparent may bring back memories of having your own children. It is worth recording those emotions, as well as the joy of less responsibility, or perhaps the concern of not wanting to be seen to interfere. Then there is the delight of grandchildren growing up, but be careful not to write too much about them. Whilst it is natural to be besotted, your book is about far more than the grandchildren and it is important not to create an imbalance.

Guarding against favouritism

Whilst such concerns also apply when writing about children, there is a greater tendency for favouritism with grandchildren, not least because you may see some of them far more than others. Obviously there will be more to write about older grandchildren, but try to be as even-handed as possible. For example, if you mention the date of birth of one, follow the same pattern for each of them.

If this is a potential problem, count the number of times each name appears – something very easy if you are using a word processor, or having your handwritten manuscript typed up at a later stage.

When including photographs in your book, care needs to be exercised to avoid creating an imbalance with too many pictures of the grandchildren. If you are limited for space, it is preferable to have older photos, like those of your grandparents, parents, yourself, siblings and spouse throughout their lives and your children growing up. If you do include several pictures of grandchildren, again, count the number of times each one appears to avoid imbalance or offence.

Retirement

Even for those who cannot wait to retire to pursue exciting new opportunities, this can also be a time of mixed emotions, particularly if it has come suddenly, for example through redundancy or ill-health, reducing any time for adjustment. Assuming that you have retired, you might like to consider:

- when you first started thinking seriously about retiring;
- what preparations were made by you and/or your company;
- if you had the opportunity to return to work part-time or as a consultant;
- what efforts were made by your employer and colleagues to mark your retirement;
- how your retirement was acknowledged or celebrated by the family;
- how you felt on your first day of actual retirement when you would normally be going to work;
- what effort was made to keep in touch with your work colleagues, either by them or yourself;
- if you did pop back to your old workplace, how you felt and the reception you received;
- how long it took you to adjust to retired life;
- what you missed about working;
- how it affected your relationship with your spouse, and what adjustments had to be made.

A new way of life

You can now go on to describe your new way of life in retirement:

- hobbies – whether you spent more time on existing hobbies or started new ones like golf, bowls, a writing circle, genealogy, bungy jumping ... or writing your life story;
- adult education classes – learning new skills like computing, painting, a foreign language, etc.;

🖎 family – spending more time with them, especially the grand-children;

🖎 part-time jobs – whether by need or by choice;

🖎 voluntary work – with all its various demands and rewards;

🖎 catching up with friends – doing some of those things you promised you would do when you had the time.

Holidays

Given the opportunity, some people start their retirement by taking that holiday they had been promising themselves for years, maybe even a trip around the world. If you kept a diary of this holiday of a lifetime, you can even include it in your book, although if it is quite lengthy it might be better as an appendix.

With low-cost winter breaks available in places like Spain and the United States, some people return year after year. If this is your experience, don't forget to include a few of your new-found friends in your book – after all, they are sure to want to read it when they find they have an author in their midst!

Concluding your book

Having brought your book up to the present day, you now have to decide how to draw it to a positive conclusion. You can be as imaginative in this as you like, but here are a few suggestions.

A family milestone

A significant family event might be the fitting conclusion to your book. Even if it was a few years ago, you are allowed some flexibility:

- your 75th birthday;
- your 50th wedding anniversary;
- your grandson's 21st birthday;
- the birth of your latest grandchild or even great-grandchild;
- your daughter's 40th birthday;
- a school reunion.

A national event

You don't have to bring the book right up to date, so you could end with the millennium, or having seen Queen Elizabeth II's coronation on television in 1953, and her Silver Jubilee in 1977, the Golden Jubilee in 2002 might be an excellent way to conclude your writing. You can even record how you celebrated each occasion, describing how the national mood has changed over the years.

Bringing a smile to the reader's face

Grandchildren have a knack of deflating self-important egos, and such words might be a fitting conclusion to your magnum opus.

'Granddad, now that you've written a book will you be worth knowing?'

A review

You might like to review the times through which you have lived and the changes you have witnessed. In this you can include some of the special people who have touched your life and made it all the richer.

Looking to the future

Readers like to feel uplifted at the end of a book, so however you decide to finish, something positive is advisable – maybe looking to the future. 'I hope that you enjoy this book, and if I receive enough good reports, who knows, I may consider writing a sequel in ten years' time … so be warned!'

Quoting from a master

You can end your book with an appropriate quotation, an inspiring song or hymn, an uplifting verse of scripture or perhaps a favourite poem … possibly even one of your own. Here's how Elspeth McKechnie concluded her book.

Case study – Elspeth McKechnie

A Nonsense Poem

The time has come, the walrus said,
We've talked of many things,
Of happiness, of sorrows and certain other things.
So now I must lay down my pen,
My final word is just AMEN.

With apologies to Lewis Carroll.

Points to ponder

- Give some thought to how you would like to end the book.
- If you wrote an introduction at the start of the project, review it in case anything has changed from your original intentions.
- Ensure you are satisfied with what you have written about the most important people in your life.

Top tips

- Check the spelling of the names of children and grandchildren and their dates of birth. If you write that the Queen's coronation was 1952 rather than 1953 no one will worry unduly, but write that Katie was born in 2002 and not 2001 and you'll never hear the end of it!

- Arrange for your manuscript to be proofread, and ensure that any sensitive areas are checked with the relevant parties before you proceed with book production.

- Ideas for editing, presenting and producing your book can be found in Writing Your Life Story, by the same author and publisher.

Major Events
of 1930–1979

Major Events of 1930

Labour Prime Minister, Ramsay MacDonald comes under pressure for allowing Britain's jobless to exceed two million.

&

Canadian newspaper magnate, Lord Beaverbrook, launches the United Empire Party with support from Tory MPs disillusioned with Stanley Baldwin's lacklustre performance against Labour.

&

In the Soviet Union Stalin imposes agricultural co-operatives and collective farms to stave off the threat of famine. Suppression of the church leads to religious persecution.

&

The world's largest airship, the R101, crashes and explodes in France, killing 44 of the 52 on board.

&

The Church of England gives cautious backing to the use of birth control.

&

Amy Johnson, at 27, becomes the first woman to fly solo from Britain to Australia.

&

Music

Hits of the year: The King's Horses
On the Sunny Side of the Street

Films

Box office hits: Little Ceasar
Animal Crackers

Books

As I Lay Dying, William Faulkner

Sport

Donald Bradman records the highest first class cricket score of 452. Then, against England, he scores the highest individual test score of 334 to help Australia win the Ashes.

☙

Amateur golfer Bobby Jones wins the Grand Slam.

☙

Uruguay win the inaugural World Cup on home soil beating Argentina 4–2.

☙

Sheffield Wednesday are League Champions, and Arsenal beat Huddersfield Town in the FA Cup Final.

☙

Lancashire win the cricket County Championship.

☙

At Wimbledon, Helen Moody beats Elizabeth Ryan and Bill Tilden beats the unseeded Wilmer Allison.

☙

Major Events of 1931

Liberals force Ramsay MacDonald's minority Labour Government to accept an all-party 'Government of Co-operation'. The austerity programme sees rioting in British cities and a mutiny in the navy.

❧

In the ensuing election MacDonald continues as Prime Minister after the National Government sweeps to victory.

❧

King Alfonso abdicates as Spain declares itself a republic. Niceto Zamora is elected as Spain's first constitutional President.

❧

The Indian problem continues. Over 200 people die after rioting in Cawnpore. Ghandi, in loincloth, is invited to tea at Buckingham Palace.

❧

Al 'Scarface' Capone is charged for tax evasion in the US.

❧

Pope Pius XI, reinforcing Catholic doctrine, speaks out against sexual liberalism.

❧

Trolley buses become a regular feature of London. Cinemas are allowed to open on Sundays.

❧

Music
Hits of the year:	Goodbye
	The Peanut Vendor
	Just One More Chance

Films
Box office hits:	City Lights
	Cavalcade
	Frankenstein
	Monkey Business

Books
The Waves, Virginia Woolf

Sport

Malcolm Campbell's *Bluebird* advances the world land-speed record to 245 mph.

❧

Arsenal win the football League Championship, and West Bromwich Albion beat Birmingham City 2–1 in the FA Cup Final.

❧

Yorkshire are cricket County Champions.

❧

The Grand National is won by *Grakle*.

❧

Cilly Aussem beats Hilde Krahwinkel at Wimbledon. Sidney Wood takes the men's title as Frank Fields withdraws.

❧

Major Events of 1932

Growing disillusionment with the economy and the Government lead to rioting and hunger marches. Four cabinet ministers resign from the National Government but MacDonald soldiers on.

&

French President, Paul Doumer, is assassinated by a Russian émigré.

&

Hitler wins 230 seats in the Reichstag and the largest single party representation, but is kept from power by a coalition government led by Franz von Papen.

&

Unrest continues in India as Ghandi is arrested.

&

Japan establishes Manchurian as a puppet state.

&

Democrat Franklin Delano Roosevelt ousts Herbert Hoover in the US presidential election.

&

American aviation hero Charles Lindberg's son is kidnapped. The ransom is paid, but after 73 days the baby is found dead in a local wood.

&

In Britain, whipping of children under the age of 14 is declared illegal.

&

The BBC establishes a new HQ in Portland Place.

&

Music
Hits of the year: Love is the Sweetest Thing
Forty-Second Street
The Sun Has Got His Hat On

Films
Box office hits: Farewell to Arms
Pack up Your Troubles
Dr Jekyll and Mr Hyde
Scarface

Books
Brave New World, Aldous Huxley

Sport

Gordon Richards breaks all records, becoming the greatest
flat-racing jockey.

❧

In the Los Angeles Olympics, Great Britain wins gold in the
800 m, the 50 km walk, and the pairs and fours rowing.

❧

Everton win the football League Championship. In the FA
Cup Newcastle United beat Arsenal 2–1.

❧

Yorkshire retain the County Championship.

❧

Forbra wins the Grand National.

❧

Wimbledon – Helen Moody (née Wills) defeats Helen
Jacobs; Henry Vines defeats 'Bunny' Austin.

❧

Major Events of 1933

A massive housing programme is announced in an effort to eradicate slums. Spending on defence is increased only months after MacDonald's planned cuts and his meeting with Mussolini.

❧

Hitler becomes Chancellor in Germany, removing Jews from office and into concentration camps. Imperfect males are sterilised, opposition parties banned and Germany withdraws from the League of Nations.

❧

Communist uprisings are experienced in Spain.

❧

In the US, President Roosevelt is wounded but survives an assassination attempt. He tackles the Depression with the National Industry Recovery Act, and Prohibition Laws are repealed.

❧

Ghandi, continuing to flout the establishment, leaves jail an emaciated figure.

❧

England is accused of 'not playing cricket' in the infamous Bodyline series against Australia.

❧

Marlene Dietrich sets the fashion of women wearing men's clothes.

❧

Music
Hits of the year: Smoke Gets in Your Eyes
Who's Afraid of the Big Bad Wolf?
Stormy Weather

Films
Box office hits: Mystery of the Wax Museum
Duck Soup
Alice in Wonderland
King Kong

Books
Down and Out in Paris and London, George Orwell

Sport

Britain beat the US in the Ryder Cup by one point.

&

Fred Perry becomes the first Briton to win the US Open
Tennis Championship.

&

Arsenal win the football League Championship. Everton
beat Manchester City 3–0 in the FA Cup Final … wearing
numbered shirts!

&

Yorkshire win the County Championship for the third
successive time.

&

Kellsboro' Jack wins the Grand National.

&

At Wimbledon Helen Moody beats Dorothy Round, and
John Crawford defeats Ellsworth Vines.

&

Major Events of 1934

Despite Britain's massive expansion programme of the RAF, Churchill still warns of weak defences.

❧

Oswald Mosley's British Union of Fascists causes trouble at demonstrations throughout England.

❧

Herbert Morrison leads London's first Labour Council.

❧

Two hundred and sixty two miners die in a pit explosion in Gresford Mine near Wrexham.

❧

Hitler becomes President of Germany. He continues to eliminate all opposition, notably in the 'Night of the Long Knives'. Heinrich Himmler is put in charge of all German concentration camps.

❧

After less than three months in power, Austrian dictator Engelbert Dollfuss is assassinated. King Alexander of Yugoslavia meets the same fate at the hand of a Croatian in Marseilles. Skirmishes start on the Italian/Abyssinian border.

❧

HMS Queen Mary is launched, and post codes are introduced by the GPO.

❧

In the US, John Dillinger is shot after many escapes from the Federal Agents. Bonnie Parker and Clyde Barrow's charmed lives also end.

❧

Music
Hits of the year: I Only Have Eyes for You
You're the Top

Films
Box office hits: The Gay Divorce
Scarlet Pimpernell
Catherine the Great
Nell Gwyn

Books
A Handful of Dust, Evelyn Waugh

Sport

Italy win the first World Cup Final in Europe, defeating
Czechoslovakia 2–1.

&

Henry Cotton becomes the first Briton for 11 years to win
golf's British Open.

&

Arsenal retain the League Championship, and Manchester
City beat Portsmouth 2–1 in the FA Cup Final.

&

Lancashire win the cricket County Championship.

&

Golden Miller wins the Grand National.

&

All-British success at Wimbledon as Fred Perry beats Jack
Crawford, and Dorothy Round beats Helen Jacobs.

&

Major Events of 1935

Stanley Baldwin becomes Prime Minister as Ramsay MacDonald resigns due to ill health. The general election later in the year sees Baldwin's Tories sweep to power over Attlee's Labour Party.

✌

Hitler's massive re-armament programme is assisted by Britain signing the Anglo-German Naval Accord.

✌

Italy invades Abyssinia amidst condemnation, but little else, from the League of Nations.

✌

The Government of India Bill gives limited rights for home rule in India.

✌

An earthquake in British Baluchistan, India, kills over 20,000 people.

✌

In the US, massive dust storms wreak havoc in the mid-west. Bruno Hauptmann is executed for the murder of the kidnapped Lindbergh baby.

✌

On the home front, the Silver Jubilee of King George and Queen Mary sees street parties all over Britain. In a new age of relative prosperity MPs call for all houses to have plumbing, the *Jaguar* is the desired motor car and Gatwick is to be Europe's most advanced airport.

✌

Music
Hits of the year: Blue Moon
Cheek to Cheek

Films
Box office hits: Top Hat
Anna Karenina
A Night at the Opera
Mutiny on the Bounty
The Bride of Frankenstein

Books
Good-Bye, Mr Chips, James Hilton

Sport

The American sprinter, Jesse Owens, breaks five world
records in one afternoon.

❦

Malcolm Campbell's *Bluebird* raises the land-speed record
to over 300 mph.

❦

Ted Drake scores all seven goals as Arsenal beat Chelsea
7–1 in a league match. Sheffield Wednesday beat West
Bromwich Albion 4–2 in the FA Cup Final.

❦

Yorkshire win the cricket County Championship.

❦

Reynoldstown wins the Grand National.

❦

Major Events of 1936

In January, the death of King George V sees the accession of Edward VIII. Months later the nation is rocked further as their new king abdicates to marry the divorcee, Wallace Simpson. King George VI is the new monarch.

❧

Prime Minister, Stanley Baldwin, refuses to meet the Jarrow marchers in London.

❧

Hitler ignores the treaties of Versailles and Locarno and invades the Rhineland.

❧

The Spanish Government faces civil war against the Restoration Movement led by General Franco.

❧

Abyssinia falls; Mussolini's Italian Empire grows.

❧

King Fuad of Egypt is succeeded by his son Farouk. Later in the year, Egypt is granted Independence from Britain.

❧

Roosevelt retains the US presidency by a massive majority.

❧

The *Spitfire* is the pride of the RAF. In Germany the *Volkswagen* is born.

❧

The Crystal Palace burns to the ground.

❧

Music
Hits of the year: When I'm Cleaning Windows
The Way You Look Tonight

Films
Box office hits: Modern Times
Showboat
The Charge of the Light Brigade

Books
Gone With the Wind, Margaret Mitchell
The Thinking Reed, Rebecca West
Eyeless in Gaza, Aldous Huxley

Sport

The Berlin Olympics are dominated by the black athlete
Jesse Owens, both for his prowess on the track and for
undermining Hitler's Aryan dream.

✄

Sunderland win the League Championship, and Arsenal
beat Sheffield United 1–0 in the FA Cup.

✄

Derbyshire win the cricket County Championship.

✄

Reynoldstown retains the Grand National.

✄

At Wimbledon Helen Jacobs defeats Hilda Sperling, and
Fred Perry defeats Von Cramm for his third successive title.

✄

Major Events of 1937

The Coronation of George VI is the major royal event of the year.

❧

In Parliament, air raid shelters in most of Britain's towns and cities are proposed, and the Green Belt Act is passed.

❧

Neville Chamberlain becomes Prime Minister.

❧

Hitler instils Nazi values in all children; parents who do not comply face the removal of their offspring. German bombers are sent to help General Franco in the Spanish Civil War. Hitler also has a new ally in Mussolini.

❧

Stalin authorises a witch-hunt to eradicate the threat of Trotskyism.

❧

The Chinese Government under Chiang Kai-shek, and Mao Tse-tung's Communists unite in a war against their common enemy, Japan.

❧

Static electricity causes the explosion of the giant airship, *Hindenburg*, killing all 33 on board.

❧

In the US, Congress passes Neutrality Laws.

❧

Hollywood star, Jean Harlow, dies at the age of 26.

❧

Music

Hits of the year: A Nice Cup of Tea
September in the Rain
The Folk Who Live on the Hill

Films

Box office hits: A Day at the Races
King Solomon's Mines
The Prisoner of Zenda
Underneath the Arches

Books

The Road to Wigan Pier, George Orwell
Out of Africa, Karen Blixen

Sport

Joe Louis defeats James Braddock to become the world
heavyweight boxing champion.

❧

Sir Malcolm Campbell raises the world water speed record
to 129 mph.

❧

Manchester City win the League Championship;
Sunderland beat Preston North End 3–1 in the FA Cup
Final.

❧

Yorkshire win the cricket County Championship.

❧

Royal Mail wins the Grand National.

❧

Dorothy Round and Donald Budge take the Wimbledon titles.

❧

Major Events of 1938

Neville Chamberlain concedes to Italy in the Anglo–Italian Agreement – Foreign Secretary, Anthony Eden resigns in protest. Chamberlain announces 'Peace in our time', appeasing Hitler over Czechoslovakia; crowds rejoice, but MPs see it as a sell-out.

&

Hitler annexes Austria in a selective election, and then encroaches into Czechoslovakia. Further Jewish persecution sees all capital confiscated and, on 9 November, 'Kristallnacht'.

&

Franco's relentless push on Madrid sees Republican Spain split in two.

&

The Japanese take Canton.

&

Tycoon aviator, Howard Hughes, flies around the world in less than four days.

&

Americans believe Martians have landed after Orson Welles' broadcast of *War of the Worlds*!

&

Glasgow hosts the King and Empire Exhibition.

&

The *Queen Elizabeth* liner is launched.

&

Steam train *Mallard* reaches record 126 mph.

&

Music

Hits of the year:　Whistle While You Work
　　　　　　　　　　Begin the Beguine
　　　　　　　　　　Alexander's Ragtime Band

Films

Box office hits:　The Adventures of Robin Hood
　　　　　　　　　The Adventures of Tom Sawyer
　　　　　　　　　Bringing up Baby
　　　　　　　　　Never Say Die
　　　　　　　　　Snow White and the Seven Dwarfs

Books

Murphy, Samuel Beckett

Sport

Italy win their second football World Cup.

❧

Arsenal win the football League Championship. In the FA Cup, Preston North End beat Huddersfield Town 1–0 after extra time.

❧

Len Hutton scores a record 364 runs as England score 903 to thrash Australia.

❧

The US take all five titles at Wimbledon, Don Budge and Helen Moody being victorious in the singles.

❧

Major Events of 1939

In April, Britain and France sign a pact with Poland to provide assistance in the event of German aggression.

&

In May, Hitler and Mussolini form a fascist alliance, the 'Pact of Steel'.

&

In August, the Soviet Union and Germany sign a 'Non-Aggression Pact', making the prospect of a European war inevitable.

&

As war approaches air raid shelters are distributed to homes in London, conscription is enforced, farmers are called to dig for victory, and children from towns and cities are evacuated to the country.

&

On 1 September Germany invades Poland. Hitler fails to respond to Chamberlain's ultimatum to suspend her attack. On 3 September Britain and France declare war on Germany. Australia, New Zealand and Canada immediately support Britain.

&

Winston Churchill and Anthony Eden are called to the 'War Cabinet' as First Lord of the Admiralty and Dominions Secretary respectively.

&

The British battleship, *Royal Oak* is sunk in the Scapa Flow. The German battleship, the *Graf Spee* is scuttled in the River Plate, after being trapped and damaged by British warships.

&

One hundred and fifty eight thousand British troops land in France.

❧

Mussolini occupies Albania.

❧

The United States declares neutrality, but allows the Allies to buy armaments and supplies.

❧

In Spain, the Civil War ends as Franco and the Nationalist forces take control.

❧

The death of Pope Pius XI sees the accession of Pope Pius XII.

Music
Hits of the year: Over the Rainbow
Washing on the Siegfried Line

Films
Box office hits: Gone with the Wind
The Wizard of Oz
The Cat and the Canary
The Four Feathers
Wuthering Heights
Beau Geste
Young Mr Lincoln
Stagecoach

Books
The Grapes of Wrath, John Steinbeck
Rebecca, Daphne du Maurier

Major Events of 1940

Germany invades Norway and Denmark for their strategic bases, from which they can attack British shipping, and for their iron ore reserves.

✎

Winston Churchill succeeds Neville Chamberlain as Prime Minister and immediately forms an all-party coalition.

✎

At Dunkirk one third of a million allied servicemen are evacuated by a flotilla of British vessels as German troops advance on Dunkirk.

✎

In the 'Battle of Britain' over the skies of southern England, the RAF rebuffs the Luftwaffe.

✎

The Blitz becomes a way of life to Londoners.

✎

France surrenders under merciless German terms, whilst a little-known French General, by the name of de Gaulle, rallies the French resistance.

✎

Holland and Belgium surrender under Hitler's blitzkrieg.

✎

Mussolini declares war on the Allies, but faces setbacks in Greece, Albania, Libya and Somaliland.

✎

Franco rebuffs Hitler's call for assistance.

&

The 14-week Russo–Finnish Winter War ends with the Soviet Union gaining a base on the Hango Peninsula – but not before they suffer vast losses, perhaps as many as one million dead.

&

Food rationing is introduced in Britain.

&

Democrat, Franklin Delano Roosevelt, returns for a record third term in office.

&

Music
Hits of the year: A Nightingale Sang in Berkeley Square
Whispering Grass

Films
Box office hits: In Which We Serve
Fantasia
The Grapes of Wrath
Pinocchio
My Little Chickadee
Rebecca

Books
For Whom the Bell Tolls, Ernest Hemingway
The Grapes of Wrath, John Steinbeck

Major Events of 1941

Bombing raids by the Luftwaffe continue in London and
spread to other major cities.

☙

Male conscription is extended from 18½ to 50 years of age,
and unmarried women between 20 and 30 are called up
for desk jobs and essential services. In the 'womanpower'
initiative, women undertake industrial and agricultural work.

☙

The 'V for Victory' campaign is launched.
The Daily Worker is banned, and price freezes are enforced
to prevent racketeering.

☙

The Atlantic Charter brings closer accord between the US
and Britain, following the American 'Lend–Lease' terms for
the duration of the war.

☙

With the Japanese attack on Pearl Harbour the United
States enters the war.

☙

Germany takes Yugoslavia, and then Athens, as the Allies
withdraw from Greece.

☙

Germany reneges on the Non-Aggression Pact with the
Soviet Union and attacks on five fronts. Stalin orders
a scorched earth policy and bombing of the Lenin-
Dnjeproges dam to slow the advance. The Germans lay
siege to Moscow, but in the extreme winter conditions the
Russians inflict a series of defeats on the Axis forces.

☙

Britain formally declares war on Hitler's puppets: Finland,
Rumania and Hungary.

❧

After *HMS Hood* is sunk by the *Bismarck*, the Allies exact
revenge by hounding and sinking the *Bismarck*.

❧

The Royal Navy traps the Italian Navy off Crete inflicting
severe losses. Later in the year, the aircraft carrier
HMS Ark Royal is sunk by an Italian U-boat.

❧

The 'desert rats' are effective in Africa against Rommel's
Afrika Korps.

❧

Music
Hits of the year: White Cliffs of Dover
Boogie-Woogie Bugle Boy

Films
Box office hits: Citizen Kane
Billy the Kid
Dr Jekyll and Mr Hyde
Dumbo
How Green was My Valley
Seawolf

Books
Blood, Sweat and Tears, Winston Churchill

Major Events of 1942

On the home front, austerity measures see the 'Plimsoll line' on baths, beetroot colouring for lipstick and cardboard wedding cakes. In order to conserve material, skirts become shorter, shirts sleeveless and trousers lose their turn-ups.

৯

Britain signs a 20-year alliance with Russia. Roosevelt promises a stronger US commitment, and Eisenhower assumes command of US forces in Europe.

৯

The Beveridge Report lays the foundation for a post-war welfare state.

৯

'Bomber Harris' co-ordinates RAF blanket bombing raids on German industrial cities, like Cologne and Dusseldorf. German reprisals hit the 'Baedeker' towns.

৯

Russians repulse the Nazi summer offensive. With increased resources, the Germans finally take Sebastopol before turning to Stalingrad. After hand-to-hand battles, the Germans are routed.

৯

At the instigation of the SS, over one million Jews are exterminated.

৯

Himmler exacts savage revenge and slaughter on Czechs for killing Hydrich.

৯

The strategic island of Malta suffers innumerable aerial attacks from the Axis forces. Despite meagre relief supplies, Malta holds out and the island is awarded the George Cross.

&

Rommel's early advances in Northern Africa are finally held at El Alamein. General Montgomery takes command of the 8th Army and overpowers the Axis forces.

&

The Nazi naval base at St Nazaire is destroyed, but many prisoners are taken. The Allied assault of Dieppe results in heavy casualties.

&

After early success, Japan is finally thwarted by the Americans. The Battle of Midway is hoped to be a turning point.

&

Music
Hits of the year: We'll Meet Again
White Christmas

Films
Box office hits: Casablanca
In Which We Serve
Mrs Miniver
Yankie Doodle Dandy
Bambi
Road to Morocco

Books
The Song of Bernadette, Franz Werfel
The Moon is Down, John Steinbeck

Major Events of 1943

In a year of diplomacy, Churchill and Roosevelt are joined by Stalin in Tehran as 'The Big Three' plan the campaign for 1944. Churchill and Roosevelt also meet Marshal Kaishek of China to discuss Japanese hostilities.

❧

General Dwight Eisenhower is placed in charge of operations in Western Europe, his 'number two' being Montgomery.

❧

One hundred and seventy eight civilians are crushed to death in a freak accident in a Bethnal Green air raid shelter. Twenty three schoolgirls die when a German bomb hits their school.

❧

In the Warsaw ghetto, Jews are massacred by Hitler's SS.

❧

The 'Bevin Boys' are the allotted 10% of able-bodied men required to work in the mines rather than fight at 'the front'. Part time work is made compulsory for all women.

❧

PAYE is introduced, and the Keynes Plan, to ensure post-war economic recovery, is announced.

❧

After many allied advances, Mussolini is deposed by Marshal Bodaglio. Within weeks Italy surrenders and joins the Allies as Germany loots and exacts revenge on Italy.

❧

The tank battle at Kursk marks the first of many victories over Germany as, town by town, Russia recaptures her territory.

❧

RAF bombing raids continue as Hamburg is razed to the ground. Barnes-Wallace's bouncing bombs destroy the Mohne and Eder dams, the resultant flooding wreaking havoc and destruction to industry.

❧

Jean Moulin, known as 'Max', leader of the French resistance, is executed.

❧

German U-boats lose their domination of the seas as radio signals are tracked and the enigma code is broken.

❧

Music
Hits of the year: You'll Never Know
Brazil

Films
Box office hits: Heaven Can Wait
Jane Eyre
Tender Comrade

Books
The Robe, Lloyd C. Douglas
Hungry Hill, Daphne du Maurier
A Tree Grows in Brooklyn, Betty Smith

Major Events of 1944

The biggest threat on the home front comes from the unmanned flying bombs, V-1 'Doodlebugs', and later in the year the more powerful V-2s.

❧

The Axis forces are pushed back on all fronts. After the Normandy landings, the Allies secure Paris, advance into Belgium and Holland and break Hitler's vital Seigfried Line. At the end of the year Germany counter-attacks in the Ardennes.

❧

Allied advances northwards gradually secure Italy, Greece is repossessed, and via the Russian offensive, Leningrad, the Crimea and the vital oil fields of Bucharest are taken. Rumania joins the Allies.

❧

Heavy allied losses are incurred in a daring attempt to capture three bridges at Nijmegen, Grave and Arnhem.

❧

MacArthur recaptures the Philippines as the Allies turn their attention to Japan. The US tries out the B-29s, the new long distance bombers.

❧

Hitler survives a bomb planted by his senior officers, who are dealt with by the People's Court; Rommel prefers suicide.

❧

Atrocities are revealed in the concentration camps.

❧

De Gaulle heads up the Free French forces.

❧

An entire French village is slaughtered in a reprisal for the killing of an SS officer by the resistance.

❧

Roosevelt is returned for a record fouth term in office.

❧

Plans are laid down for the United Nations, a post-war peace-keeping organisation.

❧

A post-war national health service, and education and building programmes are announced for Britain – including 500,000 'prefabs' for bombed-out families and demobilised servicemen. Clothing restrictions are lifted, but a 3-week miners' strike over a unified pay structure hampers the war effort.

❧

Music
Hits of the year: Mairzy Doats
There Goes that Song Again

Films
Box office hits: This Happy Breed
Ministry of Fear
Champagne Charlie
Pearl of Death

Books
Strange Fruit, Lilian Smith.
The Razor's Edge, W. Somerset Maugham

Major Events of 1945

After a mopping-up campaign, including the controversial
bombing of Dresden, Germany surrenders to the Allies
on 7 May. A week earlier, Hitler had taken his own life.
Mussolini was executed in Italy.

&

The war continues against Japan, surrender being secured
in August after the dropping of atomic bombs on the cities
of Hiroshima and Nagasaki.

&

The end of the war sees spontaneous street parties and a
2-day national holiday.

&

Countries are quick to jockey for positions in claiming the
spoils of war. Berlin is divided between Britain, Russia,
France and the United States. Much of Eastern Germany is
given to Russia, although fears spread of an 'Iron Curtain'
of Communism being erected.

&

The Nuremberg trials start, to bring the leading war
criminals to justice.

&

The world counts the cost of war: 55 million dead, and
the appalling scars bear witness to man's capacity for evil,
notably the horrors of the death camps in Germany and
Japan. German civilians are escorted around the camps to
expose the full extent of the atrocities.

&

Apparatus is put in place to ensure that slaughter on such a scale is never repeated. The United Nations is founded to oversee world peace. Other institutions formed are the International Monetary Fund and the World Bank.

&

Churchill, the wartime hero, is rejected by the electorate as their peacetime leader. Labour gains a strong majority under the premiership of Clement Attlee who announces a period of austerity ahead.

&

General Charles de Gaulle is unanimously elected as president of France.

&

In Argentina, Colonel Juan Peron becomes premier.

&

Music

Hits of the year: We'll Gather Lilacs in the Spring
My Guy's Come Back

Films

Box office hits: Blithe Spirit
The Picture of Dorian Gray
Brief Encounter
And Then There Were None
Road to Utopia
The Bells of St Mary's

Books

Animal Farm, George Orwell
Forever Amber, Kathleen Windsor

Major Events of 1946

Top Nazis are executed at the Nuremberg war trials. Ten are given death sentences, but Goering cheats the hangman by committing suicide.

૪

The Congress Party in India rejects Britain's independence plans as unrest between Muslims and Hindus escalates. Mahatma Gandhi fasts for a peaceful transition to independence in India, but more than a quarter of a million are killed.

૪

Britain returns to war-time rations as fear grows of a worldwide famine.

૪

The United Nations has its inaugural session in Westminster, with the King and the Prime Minister addressing 51 nations.

૪

The Government plans to spend £380 million on creating 20 new towns that, it is hoped, will house one million people.

૪

Heathrow Airport opens for the first civilian flights. The site only has a row of huts and some telephone boxes, but development plans are in place.

૪

Thirty three die as barriers at Bolton Wanderers' football ground fail during an FA Cup tie.

૪

The inventor of the 'Biro', Hungarian journalist Ladislao Biro, claims it can write 200,000 words without being refilled.

&

Photo-finish cameras are installed at all racecourses.

&

Television begins again after the war, and bananas appear at Covent Garden market for the first time since 1939.

&

H.G. Wells dies, aged 80.

&

Music
Hits of the year: A Gal in Calico
                            It's a Pity to Say Goodnight

Films
Box office hits: Notorious

Books
The King's General, Daphne du Maurier

Sport

The Derby, back at Epsom after 6 years, is won by *Mr Ferguson*.

&

FA Cup – Derby County beat Charlton Athletic 4–1.

&

Major Events of 1947

Lord Mountbatten is appointed last Viceroy of India to preside over partition into two states, Pakistan and India. In August the two dominions come into being.

☙

Having announced their engagement in July, Princess Elizabeth and Lieutenant Philip Mountbatten are married at Westminster Abbey on 20 November.

☙

The UK, France and the USSR open talks on the Marshall Plan for the US to extend aid to Western Europe. UK and France accept it, but Russia rejects it.

☙

Fifteen hundred coalmines are nationalised by the Labour Government. Miners are suspicious of their new managers, the National Coal Board, but the mines now belong to the nation.

☙

In the coldest winter since 1881, 20-foot snowdrifts are recorded. Due to transport problems and iced-in fishing fleets, coal and food shortages hit Britain.

☙

Jewish refugees are turned away from the UK, as tens of thousands seek new homes.

☙

Hollywood stars, including Humphrey Bogart, Gene Kelly and Danny Kaye protest against President Truman's Communist 'witch hunt'.

☙

Henry Ford, inventor of the *Ford* motor car, dies, aged 83.

⚵

Irving Berlin's *Annie Get Your Gun* and *Oklahoma* by Rodgers and Hammerstein are hits in the West End.

⚵

Music
Hits of the year: They Say it's Wonderful
Maybe it's because I'm a Londoner

Films
Box offic hits: Brighton Rock
Odd Man Out

Books
Doctor Faustus, Thomas Mann

Sport

Denis Compton scores 3,816 runs and 18 centuries in a season. In addition to representing Middlesex and England at cricket, the '*Brylcreem* boy' also plays football for Arsenal and England.

⚵

Charlton Athletic beat Burnley 1–0 in the FA Cup Final.

⚵

Derby County sign Billy Steel from Liverpool for a record transfer fee of £15,000.

⚵

Jack Kramer and Margaret Osborne win the Wimbledon titles.

⚵

Major Events of 1948

Mahatma Gandhi is assassinated on 30 January. Thousands mourn, and riots erupt as the news spreads.

☙

Communists seize power in Czechoslovakia.

☙

The new state of Israel opens its doors to all Jewish immigrants. This is not recognised by the Arab states, which are already mustering forces in response. Bombings and attacks continue, killing both Arabs and Jews.

☙

Russia imposes rigid checks on all traffic between Berlin and the Western Zones, soon resulting in a total blockade. Western Allies beat the blockade with a round-the-clock airlift.

☙

A baby boom hits the UK. With the highest birth rates for 26 years, people are catching up post-war!

☙

The railways are nationalised.

☙

The National Health Service promises 'cradle to grave' care.

☙

North Korea proclaims independence, and both US-backed South Korea and Russian-backed North Korea claim jurisdiction over all Korea.

☙

Five hundred Caribbeans arrive on *HMS Empire Windrush* to help run London's transport system and hospitals.

☙

The transistor is invented to replace the valve.

❧

The Queen gives birth to her first son, Charles Philip
Arthur George.

❧

Music
Hits of the year: It's Magic
             On a Slow Boat to China

Films
Box office hits: Hamlet
             Oliver Twist
             Abott and Costello meet Frankenstein

Books
The Big Fisherman, Lloyd C. Douglas

Sport

At the London Olympics the Americans dominate the
track with 38 gold medals.

❧

Londoner Freddie Mills becomes the world light-heavyweight champion.

❧

The world's greatest batsman, Donald Bradman, is bowled
out for a duck at The Oval. In his last test match innings, 'the
Don' fails by 4 runs to record the amazing average of 100.

❧

Major Events of 1949

Israel and Egypt sign a truce, but Egypt still refuses to recognise the state of Israel.

&

Former TV star, Eva Peron ('Evita'), is ousted from Argentina by army generals fearing her popularity.

&

The North Atlantic Treaty Organisation (NATO) is formed.

&

Mao Tse-tung proclaims China a Communist Republic.

&

The Soviet Union becomes a nuclear power and carries out a controlled atomic explosion.

&

Joseph Stalin renames Russian-controlled East Germany as the German Democratic Republic.

&

India and Ireland become republics, but whilst India stays in the Commonwealth, Ireland leaves it.

&

Drastic devaluation of the pound against the dollar (from $4.03 to $2.80) throws the currency market into turmoil.

&

Clothes rationing in the UK finally ends, although years of having to 'make do and mend' still have a strong effect on the national psyche!

&

Comet, the prototype civilian jet airliner, flies at 500 mph.

❧

Columbia and *RCA* introduce 7-inch records. They play at different speeds – 33 and 45 rpm, respectively.

❧

Music

Hits of the year: Riders in the Sky
Baby it's Cold Outside

Films

Box office hits: The Third Man
Passport to Pimilco
Kind Hearts and Coronets

Books

1984, George Orwell
The Second Sex, Simone de Beauvoir

Sport

Russian Hero wins The Grand National.

❧

Wolves beat Leicester City 3–1 to win the FA Cup.

❧

At Wimbledon, Fred Schroeder beats Jaroslav Drobny and Louise Brough beats Mrs Dupont to take the singles titles.

❧

Bobby Locke wins the Open Golf Championship after a play-off against Harry Bradshaw.

❧

Major Events of 1950

Joseph Stalin of Russia and China's Mao Tse-tung sign a
pact, effectively forming a common united front against
the world.

❧

Labour, under Clement Attlee, is returned in the general
election but with a much reduced majority.

❧

North Korea invades South Korea, starting a war that
draws in the major world powers, including British troops.

❧

Eighty die in the world's largest civilian air crash as Welsh
rugby supporters return from a match against Ireland.

❧

Petrol rationing ends after 10 years, leading to a motoring
boom. There are 4.5 million drivers on the roads.

❧

Princess Anne, the second child of Princess Elizabeth and
the Duke of Edinburgh, is born.

❧

J. Sainsbury's opens its first self-service store in Croydon.

❧

Andy Pandy appears on British TV.

❧

Frank Sinatra makes his first sell-out tour of the UK.

❧

Music
Hits of the year: Mona Lisa
                      Music! Music! Music!
                      I've Got a Lovely Bunch of Coconuts

Films
Box office hits: Harvey
                    Sunset Boulevard
                    Annie Get Your Gun

Books
The Lion, the Witch and the Wardrobe, C.S. Lewis
Sunset Boulevard, Billy Wilder

Sport

The United States beat England 1–0 in the World Cup. In the final, Uruguay defeat the host nation, Brazil, watched by a crowd of 200,000.

✒

Portsmouth win the football League Championship on goal difference from Wolverhampton Wanderers.

✒

Arsenal beat Liverpool 2–0 in the FA Cup Final.

✒

Lancashire and Surrey share the cricket County Championship.

✒

Althea Brough and John 'Budge' Patty win at Wimbledon.

✒

Major Events of 1951

The United States and Britain test atomic bombs; the US also tests the first hydrogen bomb.

❧

Julius and Ethel Rosenberg are found guilty of wartime espionage in America's first atomic bomb spy trial and are sentenced to death.

❧

Aneurin Bevan quits as Minister of Labour over plans to charge for false teeth and glasses.

❧

President Truman sacks General MacArthur after a clash over US policy in the Far East.

❧

De Valera returns to power as Irish Premier.

❧

King George VI opens The Festival of Britain on the South Bank of the Thames. In addition to the Royal Festival Hall, attractions include the Dome of Discovery and the Skylon.

❧

Britain gives the USAF permission for an airbase at Greenham Common in Berkshire.

❧

Japan officially ends World War II by signing a peace treaty with 48 other nations.

❧

After a narrow general election victory, Winston Churchill
returns as Prime Minister.

❧

Austin and *Morris* merge to become the largest UK car
manufacturer.

❧

Music
Hits of the year: Shall we Dance?
                       If

Films
Box office hits: African Queen
                      Lavender Hill Mob
                      Streetcar Named Desire

Books
From Here to Eternity, James Jones
The Cruel Sea, Nicholas Montsarrat
The Catcher in the Rye, J.D. Salinger

Sport

The Oxford boat sinks in the boat race. Cambridge win the
re-run two days later.

❧

Newcastle United beat Blackpool 2–0 in the FA Cup Final.

❧

Maureen 'Little Mo' Connolly wins the US Tennis
Championship at the tender age of 16.

❧

Major Events of 1952

King George VI dies of cancer aged 56. Three hundred
thousand people pay their last respects as his body lies in
state in Westminster Abbey. The new Queen was on safari
in Kenya when she was told the news.

&

A freak flood in Lynmouth, Devon, kills over 30 and leaves
hundreds homeless.

&

Twenty six people die at the Farnborough air show when a
prototype aircraft disintegrates into the crowd.

&

A railway disaster at Harrow leaves 112 dead in a three-
train pile up.

&

Dwight Eisenhower, former Commander-in-Chief of
Allied Forces in Europe, becomes the new US president.
Richard Nixon, at 39, becomes the youngest ever vice-pres-
ident, and the Democrat John F. Kennedy, at 35, produces
a major upset in winning the senate seat for Massachusetts.

&

Foreign Secretary Ernest Bevin states that Britain will build
her own nuclear bomb to secure a place 'at the top table'
in international affairs. The bomb is tested on 3 October
1952.

&

Eva Peron, first lady of Argentina and 'heroine of the
shirtless ones', dies of cancer at the age of 33.

&

The Queen makes her first Christmas broadcast.

❧

Derek Bentley is sentenced to hang for the murder of a policeman. His accomplice, aged 16, who fired the shots, is detained at Her Majesty's pleasure.

❧

Music
Hits of the year: I'm Singing in the Rain

Films
Box office hits: Ivanhoe
Singing in the Rain
Greatest Show on Earth

Books
The Silver Chalice, Thomas B. Costain
East of Eden, John Steinbeck
The Diary of Anne Frank

Sport

Long-distance runner, Emil Zatopek, dominates the Helsinki Olympics.

❧

Maureen 'Little Mo' Connolly aged 17, beats Louise Blough to win Wimbledon. Frank Sedgman takes the men's title.

❧

Newcastle beat Arsenal to retain the FA Cup.

❧

Major Events of 1953

The Mau Mau uprising in Kenya causes panic. Whites march through Nairobi after the murder of a European settler.

✤

Stalin dies of a cerebral haemorrhage after ruling Russia for nearly 30 years. Many weep, but those in labour camps are relieved.

✤

Nikita Khrushchev is the new Russian leader.

✤

Hurricane winds, combined with high tides, bring disaster to the UK's east coast. At least 280 people drown with more still missing.

✤

At least 128 people die when the car ferry *Princess Victoria* sinks off the coast of Ireland – she sailed with her cargo doors open.

✤

Following an uprising against Soviet rule, hundreds of German workers are killed by tanks and troops.

✤

Queen Mary, the widow of King George V, dies in her sleep.

✤

Queen Elizabeth II is crowned at Westminster Abbey, in the first televised coronation. In the UK 526,000 TV sets were bought for the occasion, and 20 million watched the event worldwide.

✤

The conquest of Everest by Edmund Hillary and Tenzing Norgay is seen as a coronation present for the new Queen.

&

As 'Smog' continues, masks are issued on the NHS.

&

James Watson and Francis Crick suggest a structure for DNA, the molecule of life.

&

The Goons attract a cult following.

&

Music
Hits of the year: Rags to Riches
                                I Love Paris
                                Diamonds are a Girl's Best Friend

Films
Box office hits: Kiss me Kate
                                Gentlemen Prefer Blondes
                                Roman Holiday
                                From Here to Eternity

Books
The High and Mighty, Ernest K. Gann

Sport

Blackpool beat Bolton 3–1 in the FA Cup.

&

Len Hutton, the first professional cricketer to captain England, helps win back the Ashes after 20 years.

&

Major Events of 1954

Senator Joseph McCarthy, who leads an anti-Communist committee making allegations against the army and the CIA, is later condemned by the senate for conduct unbecoming of a senator.

❧

Dien Bien Phu, the French fortress in Indo-China, falls to the Viet Minh after a bloody 55-day siege.

❧

British troops pull out of Suez after being in Egypt for almost 75 years.

❧

Myxomatosis decimates Britain's rabbit population. Farmers claim the virus is necessary to stop rabbits damaging crops at a cost of £50 million every year.

❧

Comet jet planes are grounded, following a series of mysterious crashes.

❧

Nine years after the end of the war, rationing finally comes to an end. Housewives ceremonially burn their rationing books.

❧

International Business Machines (*IBM*) develops a calculating machine for business use.

❧

A polio vaccine is developed and tested.

❧

American evangelist Billy Graham conducts a three month tour of the UK.

❧

Music

Hits of the year: Rock Around the Clock
Fly Me to the Moon

Films

Box office hits: Glenn Miller Story
Moby Dick
20,000 Leagues Under the Sea
Brigadoon

Books

Lucky Jim, Kingsley Amis
The Fellowship of the Ring, J.R.R. Tolkien
Lord of the Flies, William Golding

Sport

Roger Bannister runs 3 minutes 59.4 seconds to break the 'four-minute mile' barrier.

❧

Riding *Never Say Die*, Lester Piggott, at 18, becomes the youngest jockey to win The Derby.

❧

Germany beat Hungary 3–2 in the World Cup Final.

❧

In the longest ever final, Drobny defeats Rosewall to win Wimbledon.

❧

Oxford win the 100th boat race.

❧

Major Events of 1955

Winston Churchill resigns as Prime Minister and is succeeded by Sir Anthony Eden.

☙

The Communists sign the Warsaw Pact, forming an Eastern Bloc military alliance.

☙

Civil war breaks out in Saigon, South Vietnam.

☙

A national dock strike prompts a state of emergency, with over 60,000 workers involved in the stoppage.

☙

Ruth Ellis is hanged at Holloway prison for the murder of her lover, David Blakely. She is the last woman to be hanged in Britain.

☙

The Foreign Office admits that diplomats Burgess and Maclean were spies.

☙

A bus boycott in Alabama begins as blacks refuse to sit in the back of buses, despite fines of $14.

☙

A state of emergency is declared in Cyprus as tension mounts and British soldiers continue to be killed.

☙

Princess Margaret decides against marrying Group Captain Peter Townsend.

☙

Albert Einstein dies at the age of 76, and James Dean dies
in a car crash at the age of 24.

☙

Adverts are seen on British television screens as ITV provides an alternative to the BBC.

☙

Disneyland opens in California.

☙

Blue jeans become a fashion statement.

☙

Music
Hits of the year: Give Me Your Word
                       Rosemarie

Films
Box office hits: Rebel Without a Cause
                      The Dam Busters
                      To Catch a Thief

Books
Marjorie Morningstar, Herman Wouk
Auntie Mame, Patrick Dennis
Andersonville, MacKinlay Kuntor

Sport

Newcastle United, in a record tenth FA Cup Final, beat
Manchester City 3–1.

☙

Louise Brough wins her fourth singles crown at
Wimbledon. Tony Trabert takes the men's title.

☙

Major Events of 1956

Britain joins France and Israel in attempting to prevent
General Nasser from nationalising the Suez Canal. Military
confrontation results in UN intervention.

❧

Black civil rights activists fight to desegregate schools and
bus services. Riots erupt as Alabama University is forced to
admit its first black student, who is later expelled.

❧

Hungarians revolt against Soviet domination – the ensuing
suppression results in thousands of refugees.

❧

Eisenhower wins a second term in office with a larger
majority than 1952.

❧

The Duke of Edinburgh announces an award scheme for
enterprising young people.

❧

Harold Macmillan, Chancellor of the Exchequer, introduces £1 premium bonds with tax-free prizes of £1,000.
ERNIE, the computer, is unveiled.

❧

At 21, Elvis Presley, the new singing sensation, is already a
millionaire.

❧

New self-service shops appear around the country bringing
fears of over-spending.

❧

Playwright Arthur Miller marries Marilyn Monroe.

❧

Music
Hits of the year: Heartbreak Hotel
Que Sera Sera

Films
Box office hits: The Seventh Seal
Moby Dick
Reach for the Sky
High Society
The King and I

Books
Don't Go Near the Water, William Brinkley
Peyton Place, Grace Metalious

Sport

The Queen Mother's horse, *Devon Loch*, leads the Grand National, only to fall by jumping a 'phantom fence'.

✂

Australia stages a fine Olympics in Melbourne and dominates in the pool.

✂

Jim Laker takes 19 wickets – 9 for 37 and 10 for 53 – in the fourth Test against Australia.

✂

Manchester City beat Birmingham 3–1 in the FA Cup.

✂

Real Madrid win the first European Cup.

✂

Lew Hoad beats Ken Rosewall and Shirley Fry beats Angela Buxton in the Wimbledon finals.

✂

Major Events of 1957

France, Germany, Italy, Belgium, Luxembourg and
the Netherlands sign the Treaty of Rome to establish a
European Economic Community, or 'Common Market'.

✤

Attempts to decriminalize homosexuality in the UK are
rejected.

✤

Anthony Eden resigns as Prime Minister and is replaced by
Harold Macmillan.

✤

Segregation ends in Little Rock, Arkansas, as black children
are allowed into previously white schools – 1,000 paratroopers supervise.

✤

Russia launches a satellite to start the space age. *Sputnik-1*
orbits more than 500 miles above Earth. Laika the dog is
sent in another satellite.

✤

First NATO heads of government meeting allows US
nuclear bases in Europe.

✤

The Queen makes the first televised Christmas broadcast.

✤

Ninety two rail passengers die when two trains crash under
a bridge in Lewisham in thick fog.

✤

Bill Haley and the Comets set London rocking.

✤

Macmillan makes his, 'We've never had it so good' speech.

&

The 'frisbee' is invented in the US.

&

Tommy Steele is hailed as the UK's Elvis.

&

Music
Hits of the year: Love Letters in the Sand
                       All Shook Up

Films
Box office hits: Bridge Over the River Kwai
                      Lucky Jim
                      Blue Murder at St Trinians
                      Jail House Rock
                      Gunfight at the OK Coral

Books
The Scapegoat, Daphne du Maurier
On the Beach, Nevil Shute
By Love Possessed, James Gould Cozzens

Sport

American Althea Gibson is Wimbledon's first black champion, defeating Darlene Hard. Lew Hoad retains the men's title.

&

Stirling Moss wins the British Grand Prix at Aintree – the first Briton to win the title since 1923.

&

Major Events of 1958

'Busby Babes' are killed in a Munich plane crash. Eight members of the Manchester United team and eight journalists covering the match died.

&

De Gaulle is recalled as Premier to settle the French crisis over Algerian policy. He is later elected first President of the fifth Republic.

&

CND, the Campaign for Nuclear Disarmament, is founded with a rally at Westminster Central Hall.

&

Race riots flare in Britain, as white youths taunt black immigrants in Notting Hill Gate.

&

Pope Pius XII dies and is succeeded by John XXIII after twelve ballots. He is seen as progressive and has angered ultra-conservatives.

&

Thalidomide, a drug for pregnant women, results in babies with seriously malformed limbs.

&

New inventions include Laser and the hovercraft.

&

Britain's first motorway, the 8 mile Preston by-pass in Lancashire, is opened.

&

Speed limits are introduced, and the first radar speed checks operate.

&

Elvis Presley is drafted into the American Army.

&

The practice of debutantes being presented at Buckingham Palace comes to an end.

&

Music
Hits of the year: Who's Sorry Now?
Magic Moments

Films
Box office hits: Dracula
Dunkirk
Ice Cold in Alex
South Pacific

Books
Doctor Zhivago, Boris Pasternak
Lolita, Vladimir Nabokov

Sport

Garfield Sobers sets a new test match record by scoring 365 against Pakistan.

&

Brazil wins the World Cup, defeating their Swedish hosts 5–2 in the final.

&

Major Events of 1959

Batista flees, and the populist rebel leader Fidel Castro
sweeps to power in Cuba.

૭

The Dalai Lama flees to India following China's brutal
repression of the nationalists.

૭

Archbishop Makarios is elected President of the new
Republic of Cyprus.

૭

A 'cod war' develops between Iceland and Britain.

૭

Macmillan is re-elected with a great majority in the general
election. The Tories campaigned on 'Supermac's' slogan,
'You've never had it so good.'

૭

The US sends two monkeys into space as a trial for
manned space travel.

૭

Buddy Holly dies in a plane crash, and British racing driver
Mike Hawthorn dies in a car crash.

૭

The 'Mini' is launched – it cost £500 and is capable of
70 mph. Later in the year the M1 is opened.

૭

Duty free wine and spirits are allowed for travellers abroad.

૭

Music
Hits of the year: Livin' Doll
What Do You Want to Make Those Eyes
at Me For?

Films
Box office hits: Our Man in Havana
Ben Hur
Sleeping Beauty
Some Like it Hot

Books
Lady Chatterley's Lover, D.H. Lawrence

Sport

Yorkshire ends Surrey's 7-year domination of the cricket
County Championship.

❧

Nottingham Forest beat Luton Town in the FA Cup.

❧

Billy Wright wins his hundredth cap for England.

❧

Alex Olmedo of Peru beats Rod Laver and Maria Bueno
beats Dorothy Hard to take the Wimbledon titles.

❧

Major Events of 1960

At 43, John F. Kennedy, becomes the youngest man to win
a US presidential election.

&

British Tory Prime Minister, Harold Macmillan, makes his
famous 'wind of change' speech in Capetown, South Africa.

&

Fifty six black people are killed by South African police at
Sharpsville.

&

The Congo gains independence from Belgium. After
an eight-month troubled rule, 34-year-old President
Lumumba dies in mysterious circumstances.

&

The Russians shoot down an American spy plane. The pilot
receives a 10 year prison sentence.

&

National Service in Britain comes to an end.

&

The UK Government agrees to build the Thames Barrier in
London to protect against flooding.

&

Princess Margaret marries Anthony Armstrong-Jones.

&

Music
Hits of the year: Cathy's Clown
The Girl of my Best Friend

Films
Box office hits: 101 Dalmatians
Psycho
The Magnificent 7
G.I. Blues
Let's Make Love
Alamo

Books
Trustee from the Toolroom, Nevil Shute

Sport

Floyd Patterson beats Ingemar Johansson to become the
first heavyweight boxer to regain the world title.

❧

Francis Chichester sails the Atlantic, solo, in 40 days.

❧

In the Rome Olympics, gold medals go to Britons Anita
Lonsborough and Don Thompson, whilst the American,
Cassius Clay, takes the light-heavyweight boxing title.

❧

Burnley win the football League Championship, and
Wolves beat Blackburn Rovers 3–0 in the FA Cup Final.

❧

Yorkshire win the cricket County Championship.

❧

Major Events of 1961

The US breaks off diplomatic relations with Cuba.

&

Russian, Major Yuri Gagarin, becomes the first man in space. He orbited the earth and returned safely after a flight of 108 minutes.

&

Paris faces resistance from soldiers who reject an autonomous Algeria, but General de Gaulle manages to prevent a coup.

&

In a bid to overthrow Castro's Marxist Government, Cuban exiles invade the Bay of Pigs. A wave of international tension follows as President Kennedy resolves to intervene if Kruschev assists Castro.

&

Adolf Eichmann is tried for holocaust atrocities, and is later condemned to hang.

&

The Communists erect a concrete wall across Berlin to stop the swelling exodus of East Germans seeking a new life in the West.

&

Great Britain applies for membership of the EEC.

&

Dr Michael Ramsey becomes the new Archbishop of Canterbury.

&

The contraceptive pill goes on sale for the first time.

❧

Children's Hour is dropped from BBC Radio, and the Beatles appear in the Cavern Club in Liverpool.

❧

Beyond the Fringe, a revue starring Alan Bennett, Jonathan Miller, Peter Cook and Dudley Moore, attracts younger audiences but is criticised by the establishment.

❧

Music
Hits of the year: Wooden Heart
                      You Don't Know

Films
Box office hits: El Cid
                     Birdman of Alcatraz
                     West Side Story

Books
The Winter of our Discontent, John Steinbeck
To Kill a Mockingbird, Harper Lee

Sport

Tottenham Hotspur win 'the double'.

❧

Angela Mortimer beats Christine Truman in an all-British Wimbledon final. Rod Laver defeats Charles McKinley for the men's title.

❧

Major Events of 1962

The US and Russia swap spies on a Berlin bridge after months of negotiations.

☙

John Glenn becomes the first US citizen to orbit Earth. His capsule, 'Friendship', circled the earth three times before splashing down in the Atlantic.

☙

In Algeria, 132 years of French rule end as the Algerian population vote for independence.

☙

Harold Macmillan sacks seven Cabinet members 24 hours after a huge Tory voting collapse in by-election polling.

☙

The Cuban missile crisis brings the world to the brink of nuclear war. When Krushchev and Kennedy settle their differences, a huge sigh of relief is heard across the world.

☙

US troops are sent to Laos to protect vital interests in Vietnam.

☙

Nelson Mandela is jailed in South Africa for five years for organising a national strike.

☙

Emergency vaccinations are administered after an outbreak of smallpox in Yorkshire.

☙

Marilyn Monroe is found dead in her bed. She married three times and made 23 films.

❧

Live trans-Atlantic television becomes a reality as the Telstar Communications Satellite is launched.

❧

The UK and France agree to make Concorde.

❧

Music
Hits of the year: Stranger on the Shore
I Remember You
Rock a-hula Baby

Films
Box office hits: Day of the Triffids
Dr No
The Great Escape
Lawrence of Arabia

Books
Ship of Fools, Katherine Anne Porter
Dearly Beloved, Anne Morrow Lindbergh
A Shade of Difference, Allen Drury

Sport

Brazil beat Czechoslovakia 3–1 to retain the World Cup.

❧

After a seven-horse pile-up that sees four jockeys receive hospital attention, Larkspur wins the Derby.

❧

Major Events of 1963

John Profumo, Secretary of State for War, resigns after lying to the Commons over his relationship with Christine Keeler. He refutes any breach of security, despite Keeler's liaison with a Soviet naval officer.

&

Russia and the US establish a hotline phone link.

&

At a Washington peace protest, Martin Luther King proclaims 'I have a dream', affirming that all men are created equal.

&

President John F. Kennedy is assassinated in Dallas whilst driving through the city in an open car. Lee Harvey Oswald is later arrested and charged with murder, only to be shot and killed by Jack Ruby.

&

'The Great Train Robbery' nets £2.6 million and prompts a nationwide hunt.

&

In Europe, France vetos Britain's entry into the EEC, and a nuclear test ban treaty is agreed.

&

Kenya gains independence.

&

Beatlemania continues to take the UK pop world by storm.

&

Music
Hits of the year: She Loves You
                      From Me to You
                      In Dreams

Films
Box office hits: Cleopatra
                      The Greatest Story Ever Told
                      Billy Liar
                      The Birds
                      From Russia with Love
                      The Pink Panther

Books
The Glass-Blowers, Daphne du Maurier

Sport

In beating Athletico Madrid 5–1, Spurs are the first British
team to win the European Cup Winner's Cup.

✤

British heavyweight champion, Henry Cooper, gives
Cassius Clay a fright. He knocks down the world
champion, but has to retire with a badly cut eye.

✤

At Wimbledon Chuck McKinley beats Fred Stolle and
Margaret Smith beats the promising teenager, Billie-Jean
Moffitt.

✤

Major Events of 1964

Brezhnev replaces Khruschev in a Kremlin coup.

❧

The Prime Minister of India, Jawaharial Nehru, dies at the
age of 74.

❧

Following attacks on US destroyers, Lyndon Johnson gets
Congress backing to take all necessary action against the
Communist regime in North Vietnam.

❧

Harold Wilson becomes Britain's first Labour
Prime Minister since Attlee.

❧

Twelve members of the great train robbery gang are
sentenced to a total of 307 years in jail.

❧

'Mods' and 'Rockers' clash at seaside resorts in the UK
throughout the summer, including Brighton, Margate,
Southend and Clacton.

❧

As Beatlemania hits the US, 'pirate' stations,
Radio Caroline and Radio Atlanta, broadcast pop music to
the youth of Britain.

❧

Nelson Mandela is sentenced to life imprisonment in
South Africa.

❧

MPs vote to abolish the death penalty.

❧

Steptoe and Son is Britain's most popular TV show, whilst *The Avengers* is a rising star.

❧

Britain and France agree to build Channel tunnel.

❧

Music
Hits of the year: I Love You Because
                   I Won't Forget You

Films
Box office hits: A Hard Day's Night
                 Goldfinger
                 Mary Poppins
                 My Fair Lady

Books
The Spy Who Came in from the Cold, John le Carré
You Only Live Twice, Ian Fleming

Sport

The United States dominate the Tokyo Olympics.

❧

Cassius Clay surprises the boxing world by defeating Sonny Liston to become Heavyweight Champion.

❧

Major Events of 1965

Sir Winston Churchill dies at the age of 90. His body lies
in state at Westminster Hall, and live television coverage of
the funeral attracts a record worldwide audience.

&

In addition to bombarding North Vietnam, the US sends
Marines into the country in support of South Vietnam to
fight the Communist aggressor.

&

India invades Pakistan as the conflict over Kashmir
escalates. Harold Wilson sees this as the greatest threat to
world peace since World War II.

&

Ian Smith, Prime Minister of Rhodesia, the last British
colony in Africa, declares independence.

&

Ian Brady and Myra Hindley are charged with the
'Moors Murders'.

&

The Post Office Tower, the tallest building in the UK, is
opened, with a revolving circular restaurant at the top.

&

Mary Whitehouse sets up the National Viewers' and
Listeners' Association to clean up radio and TV.

&

The Beatles receive MBEs, much to the chagrin of the
establishment.

&

Miniskirts are all the rage – tax rules are changed to prevent them being passed off as children's skirts, and so be exempt from tax.

&

Goldie, the Golden Eagle, achieves national fame. Escaping from London Zoo, he causes traffic jams as motorists stop and stare.

&

Music
Hits of the year: Tears
                       A Walk in the Black Forest

Films
Box office hits: The Sound of Music
                      Dr Zhivago

Books
Herzog, Saul Bellow
The Man with the Golden Gun, Ian Fleming

Sport

Liverpool win the FA Cup for the first time, beating Leeds United in extra time.

&

Sir Stanley Matthews retires from football.

&

Major Events of 1966

Under Chairman Mao, China experiences its 'Cultural Revolution'. Students are formed into groups of Red Guards and the Little Red Book becomes required reading.

&

The United States continues its military offensive in Vietnam.

&

The Pope and the Archbishop of Canterbury hold an historic meeting – the first for 400 years.

&

In the US, a peace protester is shot on a civil-rights march, leading to race riots.

&

One hundred and sixteen children and 28 adults are killed in the small Welsh mining village of Aberfan when a slag heap collapses and buries the local school.

&

The breath-test is introduced on Britain's roads.

&

The Farnborough Air Show sees the first appearance of the Hawker Harrier jump-jet which can take off and land vertically.

&

Freddie Laker's travel company offers cheap flights and holiday packages.

&

The King's Road and Carnaby Street become the epicentre of London fashion, British rock is popular worldwide, and *Time* magazine declares 1966 as the year of 'Swinging London'.

❧

Music
Hits of the year: Strangers in the Night
                        Day Tripper

Films
Box office hits: Alfie

Books
Valley of the Dolls, Jacqueline Susann
Human Sexual Response, Masters and Johnston

Sport

England beat Germany 4–2 to win the World Cup. The final goal was scored in the dying seconds of extra time, and the whole team, led by Bobby Moore, became national heroes.

❧

Arkle wins the Cheltenham Gold Cup for a record third time in a row.

❧

Manuel Santana and Billie-Jean King triumph at Wimbledon.

❧

Major Events of 1967

Israel seizes land from the Arabs in the 6-day war. The Gaza Strip, Bethlehem, Jordan, Jericho and the West Bank all fall to Israeli paratroopers – casualties exceed 100,000.

❧

The Vietnam War continues, as anti-war protests across the US become more widespread.

❧

As abortion is legalised and homosexual practices decriminalized, protestors fear over-liberalization of British society.

❧

Che Guevara is killed. An inspiration to guerilla groups across South America, 'Che' was formerly a confidant of Castro.

❧

Three American astronauts die on the launch pad as fire engulfs their spacecraft.

❧

Donald Campbell dies attempting to break the world water speed record on Lake Coniston. *Bluebird* leapt into the air approaching 276 mph.

❧

The *QE II* liner is launched at Clydebank.

❧

In South Africa, Dr Christiaan Barnard performs the first human heart transplant.

❧

Music
Hits of the year: Sergeant Pepper's Lonely Hearts Club Band
Release Me
There Goes Everything
Whiter Shade of Pale

Films
Box office hits: The Jungle Book
The Graduate
Bonnie and Clyde
Casino Royale
The Dirty Dozen

Books
Rosemary's Baby, Ira Levin
100 Years of Solitude, Gabriel Garcia Marquez

Sport

British cyclist Tommy Simpson dies during the Tour de
France.

&

Foinavon wins the Grand National at odds of 100–1.

&

Billie-Jean King and John Newcombe win titles at
Wimbledon.

&

In refusing military service, Muhammad Ali (formerly
Cassius Clay) is stripped of his world heavyweight boxing
titles.

&

Major Events of 1968

As the Vietnam War continues, anti-war protests erupt across the world. Peace talks start, and Lyndon Johnson orders the bombing to stop.

❧

Civil-rights campaigner Martin Luther King is assassinated. Race riots break out across the US, and the National Guard is called out.

❧

Richard Nixon becomes the new US President.

❧

Student protests in Paris lead to riots, workers strike and Communist politicians call for the resignation of President de Gaulle. However, de Gaulle wins the election.

❧

Soviet tanks roll into Prague after Czech leader Dubček introduces reforms that Russia feared would lead to the re-introduction of Capitalism.

❧

US Senator, Bobby Kennedy is assassinated.

❧

Enoch Powell makes his 'River of Blood' speech about race relations – the Tory party quickly distance his comments.

❧

The Pope says that birth control is against God's will, banning 530 million Catholics from using the pill.

❧

First and second-class stamps are introduced to the British postal system.

&

Britain sees the arrival of its first sextuplets after the use of fertility drugs.

&

Tony Hancock takes his life.

&

Music
Hits of the year: I Pretend
Wonderful World

Films
Box office hits: Chitty Chitty Bang Bang
Bullitt

Books
Airport, Arthur Hailey
Couples, John Updike

Sport

Manchester United win the European Cup, beating Benfica 4–1 in extra time.

&

Basil d'Oliveira's selection for the MCC results in South Africa banning the cricket tour.

&

Clenched fist salutes by US 'Black Power' athletes mar the Mexico Olympics in which Bob Beamon smashes the long jump record by almost 2 ft.

&

Major Events of 1969

As violence escalates in Northern Ireland, British troops are
sent in to guard key sites.

&

Mid-Ulster elects 22-year-old Bernadette Devlin to be their
MP.

&

By April the US death toll in Vietnam reaches 33,641.

&

Yasser Arafat becomes the leader of the Palestinian
Liberation Organisation.

&

Israel elects Golda Meir as Prime Minister.

&

On 21 July, Neil Armstrong sets foot on the moon,
proclaiming, 'That's one small step for a man, one giant
leap for mankind.' 'Buzz' Aldrin and Mike Collins
complete the three-man team.

&

Muammar Gaddafi leads a revolution in Tripoli and seizes
power of Libya.

&

The investiture of Prince Charles as Prince of Wales is
conducted at Caernarfon Castle.

&

The Kray twins, infamous London gang leaders, receive life
sentences for murder.

&

John Lennon marries Yoko Ono – their honeymoon is a
'bed-in' at an Amsterdam hotel.

❧

Concorde, the world's first supersonic airliner, takes her
maiden flight.

❧

Music
Hits of the year: My Way
                       Gentle on my Mind

Films
Box office hits: Butch Cassidy and the Sundance Kid
                      Kes
                      Hello Dolly

Books
The Godfather, Mario Puzo
The Andromeda Strain, Michael Crichton

Sport

The South African Springbok rugby team face anti-
apartheid protesters at Twickenham.

❧

Ann Jones beats Billie-Jean King to become only the
second British Wimbledon champion since the war.

❧

Tony Jacklin becomes the first Briton to win the British
Open since 1951.

❧

Jackie Stewart is motor racing's World Champion.

❧

Major Events of 1970

The Tories, under Edward Heath, surprisingly defeat Harold Wilson in the June election. Labour is accused of complacency.

&

President Nixon sends US troops to attack Communist bases in Cambodia.

&

The Nigerian Government crushes the Biafran revolt, in the process causing bitter recriminations about the treatment of the Biafran prisoners of war.

&

Three jet planes are blown up by Arab hijackers in the Jordanian desert. The hostages are released after Britain exchanges a terrorist.

&

Charles de Gaulle, architect of modern France, dies.

&

The Beatles split up in April – having dominated the pop world for most of the 1960s.

&

The world holds its breath as the Apollo 13 space mission is crippled by an explosion. After 4 days the craft and its three crew return safely.

&

A tidal wave kills over 150,000 in East Pakistan.

&

The first Jumbo Jet lands at Heathrow in January. The *Pan Am Boeing 707* carries 362 passengers.

&

Music
Hits of the year: Yellow River
The Wonder of You
In the Summertime

Films
Box office hits: The Railway Children
Love Story
Catch 22

Books
Love Story, Erich Segal
The French Lieutenant's Woman, John Fowles

Sport

Brazil win the World Cup, defeating Italy 4–1 in the final in Mexico City.

✿

Tony Jacklin wins the US Golf Open – the first British champion for 50 years.

✿

Everton easily win the League Championship, by nine points from Leeds United.

✿

Kent win the cricket County Championship.

✿

Gay Trip wins the Grand National.

✿

At Wimbledon John Newcome defeats Ken Rosewall, and Margaret Court defeats Billie-Jean King.

✿

Major Events of 1971

Jean-Claude 'Baby Doc' Duvalier, a 19-year-old law student, succeeds his father, Francois 'Papa Doc' Duvalier as President of Haiti.

❧

Charles Manson and three of his 'family' are sentenced to death for the Tate murders.

❧

Idi Amin ousts Milton Obote to become president of Uganda.

❧

Pakistan experiences a bloody civil war, with the army killing hundreds, and thousands more fleeing the area. In December India defeats Pakistan in a 2-week war.

❧

In Northern Ireland, the first British soldier is killed. Internment without trial begins, causing riots throughout Ulster. The IRA plans to bomb the British mainland. In the autumn the troubles claim their 100th victim, and in October the Post Office Tower is bombed.

❧

Decimalisation puts an end to pounds, shillings and pence. Most fear that shops will use this as an excuse to increase prices.

❧

Margaret Thatcher, as Education Secretary, puts an end to free school milk.

❧

Apollo 15 astronauts go for the first lunar buggy ride. TV pictures of the journey are relayed to Earth.

෧

Sixty six people die at Glasgow's Ibrox Park Stadium when barriers collapse.

෧

The Americans buy the 'wrong' London Bridge, which is erected brick by brick in Arizona.

෧

Music
Hits of the year: My Sweet Lord
      Maggie May
      Chirpy, Chirpy, Cheap, Cheap

Films
Box office hits: Bedknobs and Broomsticks
      A Clockwork Orange
      The French Connection

Books
Wheels, Arthur Hailey
The Betsy, Harold Robbins

Sport

Arsenal win the League and FA Cup double.

෧

Princess Anne wins Sports Personality of the Year.

෧

Edward Heath wins the Admirals Cup in *Morning Cloud*.

෧

Major Events of 1972

After napalm bombing of Vietnam, American ground troops are eventually withdrawn. Over 45,000 American soldiers died in the conflict, but the bombing continues.

&

In Munich, Arab terrorists storm the Israeli Olympic compound, suspending the Games. All nine hostages die during a gun battle at the airport.

&

President Nixon is re-elected, despite growing concerns over the arrest of five men attempting to bug Democrat offices in the Watergate buildings.

&

Britain's miners strike over pay and conditions, resulting in nationwide blackouts.

&

Thirteen demonstrators are shot dead by British troops in what becomes known as 'Bloody Sunday'. The Northern Ireland Government resigns after Edward Heath announces the commencement of direct rule from Westminster. Seven die in the IRA bombing of a paratroopers' HQ in Aldershot.

&

A *Trident* crashes at Heathrow, killing all 118 on board.

&

Britain joins the EEC, along with Ireland, Denmark and Norway.

&

For the first time, female students are allowed into five of Oxford's all-male colleges for a test period.

❧

Clive Sinclair invents the pocket calculator.

❧

Jesus Christ Superstar becomes a hit in the West End, despite pickets from religious groups.

❧

Music
Hits of the year: Amazing Grace
Puppy Love

Films
Box office hits: Last Tango in Paris
Cabaret
The Godfather

Books
The Odessa File, Frederick Forsyth
The Winds of War, Herman Wouk

Sport

Rangers win the European Cup Winner's Cup, beating Moscow Dynamo 3–0.

❧

At the Munich Olympics, America's Mark Spitz wins seven gold medals in the pool. The USSR's elfin gymnast, Olga Korbut, captivates audiences, and Mary Peters takes gold in the women's pentathlon.

❧

Major Events of 1973

A conference in Paris agrees peace for Vietnam. Fighting stops, Americans and Vietnamese exchange POWs, and US troops are withdrawn.

☙

In the Watergate scandal, White House aides are found guilty of conspiracy, and as a Senate committee investigates it becomes clear that Nixon knew about the cover-up.

☙

In the Middle East the Yom Kippur war between Israel and Egypt cuts off oil supplies to the UK.

☙

An economic crisis, coal strikes and the high price of oil result in Edward Heath introducing a 3-day working week to restrict energy use.

☙

Willie Whitelaw manages to get North and South to agree to a power-sharing executive for Ulster. Meanwhile, IRA terrorists hijack a helicopter and 'spring' three IRA leaders.

☙

Princess Anne marries Captain Mark Philips.

☙

Jeans are now the fashion must-have.

☙

Russian supersonic airliner, 'Concordski', crashes at the Paris air show, killing 15 people.

☙

Music
Hits of the year: Tie a Yellow Ribbon
Welcome Home
Eye Level

Films
Box office hits: The Sting
American Graffiti
Live and Let Die
Jesus Christ Superstar

Books
Jonathan Livingston Seagull, Richard Bach
The Honorary Consul, Graham Greene

Sport

Tennis stars boycott Wimbledon over contract disputes.
With 13 of the 16 male seeds missing, Jan Kodes beats Alex
Metreveli. Billie-Jean King beats Chris Evert to take the
women's title.

❧

By beating Leeds, Sunderland become the first second-divi-
sion team to win the FA Cup for 42 years.

❧

British boxer, Joe Bugner, fails to defeat Muhammad Ali for
the world heavyweight title.

❧

Red Rum wins the Grand National in a record time of
9 minutes 1.9 seconds.

❧

Major Events of 1974

Threatened with impeachment, President Nixon resigns over the Watergate scandal. Gerald Ford is sworn in as President.

વ

Russian writer Alexander Solzhenitsyn is exiled for publishing accounts of Soviet labour camps, and defects to West Germany. Ballet dancer, Mikhail Baryshnikov, defects to Canada whilst on tour in Toronto.

વ

Republican prisoners run riot in the Maze Prison. Seventeen die as two Birmingham pubs are bombed by the IRA.

વ

Outside Paris a *DC-10* crashes, killing all 344 passengers in the world's worst air disaster.

વ

India announces it has nuclear weapons.

વ

Harold Wilson becomes the new Labour Prime Minister. He wins a second general election later in the year, but with a narrow majority.

વ

A Japanese soldier walks out of the Philippine jungle and gives himself up – no one told him that the war ended 19 years before.

વ

A kidnap attempt on Princess Anne in the Mall is thwarted.

વ

Lord Lucan disappears, as police hope to question him concerning the murder of his nanny.

❧

London Zoo welcomes the giant pandas Chia-Chia and Ching-Ching.

❧

Music
Hits of the year: Seasons in the Sun
                        Tiger Feet

Films
Box office hits: Blazing Saddles
                  All Creatures Great and Small
                  Murder on the Orient Express
                  The Man with the Golden Gun

Books
Watership Down, Richard Adams
The Dogs of War, Frederick Forsyth
Jaws, Peter Benchley

Sport

Chris Evert and her fiancé, Jimmy Connors, win the Wimbledon titles.

❧

The home side, West Germany, win the World Cup, beating Holland 2–1.

❧

John Conteh becomes the first British light-heavyweight world champion for 25 years.

❧

Major Events of 1975

After a 3½ month siege, Communist Khmer Rouge forces take the capital of Phnom Penh as their leader, Pol Pot, controls Cambodia.

❧

The North Vietnamese take Saigon's presidential palace to end the Vietnam War as US embassy staff struggle to board helicopters.

❧

Violence escalates in Beirut between Christians and Muslims.

❧

In London's worst underground disaster 35 people are killed as a tube train runs into the buffers at Moorgate Station.

❧

Margaret Thatcher is elected leader of the Tories, the first female leader of a British political party.

❧

In a referendum, 67% of the British people vote to stay in the European Common Market.

❧

In June the first oil from the North Sea is brought ashore in Scotland, and later in the year the Queen opens a North Sea pipeline.

❧

Across Britain, it is estimated that over 6.5 million trees have been killed by Dutch Elm Disease.

❧

Radio pagers, 'bleepers', hit London.

✧

Charlie Chaplin is knighted, and a small firm called
Microsoft is founded.

✧

Music
Hits of the year: Bye Bye Baby
                       Sailing

Films
Box office hits: Jaws
                      The Rocky Horror Picture Show
                      One Flew Over the Cuckoo's Nest

Books
The Eagle has Landed, Jack Higgins
Shogun, James Clavell

Sport

The West Indies defeat Australia in Cricket's first
World Cup Final.

✧

New Zealander John Walker becomes the first man to run a
mile in 3 minutes 50 seconds.

✧

Czechoslovakian tennis star Martina Navratilova defects to
the US.

✧

Major Events of 1976

Jimmy Carter wins office after a television debate
embarrasses out-going President Gerald Ford.

❧

An era comes to an end as Chairman Mao dies, and a
struggle for power in China begins.

❧

Riots in the South African township of Soweto result in
over 100 deaths.

❧

Prime Minister, Harold Wilson, resigns after 13 years
as leader of the Labour Party. His successor is James
Callaghan.

❧

The first commercial flights of Concorde take place from
London and Paris.

❧

In Britain's hottest summer for 200 years, water is rationed
and forest fires sweep the country.

❧

Over 500 are injured in race riots at the Notting Hill
Carnival.

❧

A pile of bricks is the latest exhibit at the Tate Gallery.

❧

This year sees the deaths of Dame Agatha Christie,
L.S. Lowry and Howard Hughes.

❧

Music
Hits of the year: Save your Kisses for me

Don't go Breaking my Heart

Films
Box office hits: The Omen

Rocky

Books
The Deep, Peter Benchley

Sleeping Murder, Agatha Christie

Sport

African nations boycott the Montreal Olympics due to New Zealand's rugby links with South Africa. Nadia Comaneci, 14, stars in the gymnastics, whilst British swimmer, David Wilkie, wins gold and silver.

ℋ

In the Winter Olympics, British skater John Curry wins gold in the men's figure skating.

ℋ

Lester Piggott wins The Derby for the seventh time.

ℋ

Briton, James Hunt, becomes the Formula One Motor Racing Champion after beating Niki Lauda, who had been badly scarred in an accident earlier in the year.

ℋ

At the age of 20, Bjorn Borg becomes the youngest Wimbledon tennis champion for 45 years.

ℋ

Major Events of 1977

In Uganda, Idi Amin continues his reign of terror by
murdering Archbishop Luwum.

☙

In the Canary Islands two jumbo jets collide, killing 574 in
the world's worst aeroplane disaster.

☙

Street parties are held throughout the country to celebrate
the Queen's Silver Jubilee.

☙

Black civil rights activist, Steve Biko, is tortured to death at
the hands of South African police.

☙

Thousands of Vietnamese 'boat people' attempt to escape
the Communist regime.

☙

Elvis Presley is found dead at his Memphis home,
Graceland. A drug overdose is suspected.

☙

At Mogadishu airport, German anti-terrorist troops storm
a hijacked plane, killing the Palestinian terrorists but
freeing the hostages.

☙

Eleven-year-old Nigel Short becomes the youngest ever
qualifier for a national chess championship.

☙

Charlie Chaplin dies at the age of 88.

☙

Music
Hits of the year: Don't Cry For Me, Argentina
                      Don't Give Up On Us
                      When I Need You

Films
Box office hits: Star Wars
                     Saturday Night Fever
                     The Spy Who Loved Me

Books
The Thorn Birds, Colleen McCullough

Sport

Red Rum becomes the first horse to win the Grand
National three times.

✂

Liverpool win the European Cup in Rome and the League
Championship, but lose to Manchester United in the
FA Cup Final.

✂

Virginia Wade wins the Wimbledon Women's Singles
Championship in the Queen's Silver Jubilee year.

✂

Playing the Australians on his Headingley home ground,
Geoff Boycott scores his hundredth century.

✂

Major Events of 1978

The super-tanker, *Amoco Cadiz*, spills 220,000 tons of oil into the Channel, endangering marine and coastal life in Britain and France.

❧

At Camp David, Jimmy Carter brings together the leaders of Egypt and Israel for peace talks. The settlement results in Sadat and Begin sharing the Nobel Peace Prize, although disagreement remains.

❧

As Rhodesia's civil war continues 12 British missionaries are bludgeoned to death. Rhodesian forces kill over 1,200 guerrillas in 4 days alone.

❧

Pope John Paul dies after 33 days in office. A Polish Cardinal, Karol Wojtyla, becomes Pope John-Paul II.

❧

In Guyana, 913 members of the cult, 'the People's Temple', commit mass suicide using cyanide.

❧

The Shah of Iran imposes martial law, but millions march and clamour for the return of Khomeini.

❧

Louise Brown, the world's first 'test tube baby' is born in Manchester.

❧

In the 'Winter of Discontent' a number of key trade unions go on strike.

❧

Music
Hits of the year: Rivers of Babylon
You're the One that I Want
Summer Nights

Films
Box office hits: Superman
Midnight Express
Grease

Books
Chesapeake, James A. Michener
War and Remembrance, Herman Wouk

Sport

The Ryder Cup, traditionally a battle between US and UK
golfers, is opened to Europeans.

&

All-rounder Ian Botham, 22, helps England beat Pakistan
by scoring a century and taking 8 for 34.

&

Argentina beat Holland 3–1 to win the World Cup.

&

Bjorn Borg wins his third successive Wimbledon title.

&

Daley Thompson wins gold in the decathlon at the
Commonwealth games.

&

Major Events of 1979

In Iran, the Shah is driven into exile, and Ayatollah Khomeini returns to form an Islamic republic.

The Vietnamese seize power in Cambodia from the Khmer Rouge and occupy Phnom Penh.

Across the UK rubbish piles build up as strikes continue.

An IRA bomb kills Tory MP Airey Neave as he leaves the House of Commons car park. Later in the year, Lord Mountbatten is killed on his fishing boat by an IRA bomb.

Three-Mile Island nuclear reactor experiences a leak and families within 5 miles are evacuated.

Wales' rejection of devolution and Scotland's weak support leaves the constitution unchanged.

Evidence of mass murders under Pol Pot emerges as Cambodia's 'killing fields' are revealed.

Russia invades Afghanistan.

The USSR and USA sign the SALT-2 treaty to limit each super-power's arsenal of nuclear weapons.

US spacecraft *Voyager I* reveals rings around Jupiter, as well as Saturn.

❧

Margaret Thatcher becomes Britain's first woman Prime Minister as the Tories sweep to power.

❧

Music
Hits of the year: Bright Eyes
Heart of Glass
We Don't Talk Anymore

Films
Box office hits: The Deer Hunter
Monty Python's Life of Brian
Apocalypse Now

Books
The Maltese Circle, Robert Ludlum
Smiley's People, John le Carré

Sport

Nottingham Forest win the European Cup.

❧

Steve Ballesteros wins the British Open, only the second continental European to claim the title.

❧

Sebastian Coe sets new world records for the 800 m, the mile, and the 1500 m.

❧

If you want to know how…

- ❧ to buy a home in the sun and let it out
- ❧ to move overseas and work well with the people who live there
- ❧ to get the job you want, in the career you like
- ❧ to plan a wedding and make the Best Man`s speech
- ❧ to build your own home or manage a conversion
- ❧ to buy and sell houses, and make money from doing so
- ❧ to gain new skills and learning at a later time in life
- ❧ to empower yourself and improve your lifestyle
- ❧ to start your own business and run it profitably
- ❧ to prepare for your retirement and generate a pension
- ❧ to improve your English or write a PhD
- ❧ to be a more effective manager and a good communicator
- ❧ to write a book and get it published …

… if you want to know how to do all these things and much, much more …

howtobooks

If you want to know how … to write your life story

'Biographies are not only for celebrities. "Normal" people's lives – your own, in fact – can be so much more fascinating. Experience the joy and fulfilment of writing about yourself, and produce a unique record for years to come.

'The intention of this book is to help you celebrate your life and those who have been special to you. So, whether you want to write for yourself or for others, have a go – you'll be glad you did.'

Michael Oke

Writing Your Life Story
How to record and present your memories for friends and family to enjoy
Michael Oke

'Mike Oke believes passionately that everyone has within them a marvellous story – the tale of their life. He's just the man to help you tell it' – *Neil Patrick, Yours Magazine*

'This guide will show you how to research, structure, write, present and produce your material in book form. The result will be hugely satisfying.' – *Insight*

'Every aspect of the task is explained, from initial jottings to arranging for the final printing and binding of your book, even if it is only one copy to be passed round amongst friends and relatives. I would highly recommend this book.' – *Writers' Bulletin*

'Making a professional job of your autobiography is a very worthwhile project and *Writing Your Life Story* will help you make a polished job of it.' – *Writing Magazine*

ISBN 1 85703 695 6

If you want to know how ... to write short stories and articles

'Newspapers and magazines are two of the most attainable markets for article and short story writers keen to see their work in print.

'This book takes you step by step through the techniques of writing both articles and short stories. It shows you how to write to length and style, how to adapt your work for different markets and how the inclusion of fiction techniques can enhance and improve factual articles. Research and the importance of factual accuracy in fiction will be explained and guidance is given on how to present and market your finished manuscripts.

'Master the requirements of both genres and you will double your chances of writing successfully for newspapers and magazines.'

Adèle Ramet

Writing Short Stories and Articles
How to get your work published in newspapers and magazines
Adèle Ramet

'Full of ideas and specific suggestions for successful writing ... plenty of advice for the newer writer and much to jog the memory of the more experienced' – *Writers' Bulletin*

'If you are so far unpublished and are seeking to get established, then this is a book that will take you several steps forward.' – *Writers' News*

'Everything a beginner needs to know, but just as helpful for experienced writers, who will pick up all sorts of useful hints.' – *Alison Chisholm, BBC Radio*

ISBN 1 85703 949 1

If you want to know how ... to succeed at creative writing

'Do you dream of writing short stories, novels, articles or non-fiction books and getting your work published? This book shares top tips on how to create believable characters, colourful settings, gripping dialogue, intriguing plots and how to put a fresh slant on all your work.

'There is also advice and guidance on how to turn your writing into a marketable commodity for, even though many people set out to write purely for their own pleasure, there is little doubt that nothing can compare to the thrill of having work accepted for publication and reading it from a printed page.'

Adèle Ramet

Creative Writing
Unlock your imagination, develop your writing skills and get your work published
Adèle Ramet

'This is a book which merits a place on every writer's bookshelf.'
– *Writers' Bulletin*

'... an excellent book for the beginning writer. Packed with examples and case studies, this is not a book that just deals in theory.'
– *Writers' News*

ISBN 1 85703 975 0

If you want to know how ... to exercise your ability to write creatively

'If writing is one of your favourite things and, in doing it, you wish to recapture that sense of spontaneity and fun you had in childhood – this is the book for you. Its wide variety of exercises and visualisation techniques will enable you to explore the treasures of your subconscious, revisit your childhood world of games and make-believe and bring back what you find. It also suggests ways of using time, space and equipment creatively. By combining the practical with the imaginative in this way, it will help you at every stage of the writing process. Its aim is to get you writing, keep you writing and enable you to enjoy your work to the full.'

Cathy Birch

Awaken the Writer Within
Release your creativity and find your true writer's voice
Cathy Birch

'There is a solid, practical base to this book ... Give Cathy's methods a try, you might surprise yourself.' – *Writers' Bulletin*

'The book exudes confidence and optimism ... full of devices to make the imagination flow.' – *Alison Chisholm, BBC Radio*

'Your true writer's voice is unlikely to inhabit the realms of logic ... this book takes you on a journey into the subconscious to help you find that voice – and use it. The results can be both amazing and satisfying.' – *Writer's Own*

ISBN 1 85703 656 5

If you want to know how … to write and sell your novel

'The old adage about writing being ninety-nine per cent perspiration and one per cent inspiration is certainly true. Many a talented writer has failed to achieve full potential because of a lack of perspiration … or because of a lack of instruction. Writers need all the help they can get in the way of professional expertise and general advice. This book may well pinpoint just what you need to know. Read, adapt, and apply. Then try again. And don't be discouraged. If you have the one per cent inspiration, it will eventually win through.'

From the foreword by Diane Pearson,
best-selling novelist, editor at Transworld Publishers
and President of The Romantic Novelists' Association

Write and Sell Your Novel
The beginner's guide to writing for publication
Marina Oliver

"… an excellent introduction for the new novelist." – *Writing Magazine*

"What I like about Marina's approach is the emphasis she places on characterisation … she shows how to make the characters compelling, how to keep the pages turning … The book is packed full of short and pithy tips, taking on board quotes from editors and agents. There isn't one piece of advice, one tip or suggestion for further reading that isn't full of practical common-sense." – *Writers' Bulletin*

ISBN 1 85703 876 2

If you want to know how … to get your writing published

'Publishers need writers. Without writers there would be nothing for them to publish. If you can offer quality work to the right market at the right time, you'll have as good a chance of success as anyone.'

Chriss McCallum

The Writers' Guide to Getting Published
Chriss McCallum

This book focuses on advising aspiring writers on how to achieve their dream of getting into print, whatever their writing interests. It covers many different types of publication, from mainstream magazines and newspapers through to the radio and the Internet, and reveals how best to complete letters to publishers, and create layouts, outlines and synopses for proposals. It shows you how to be a successful writer by balancing your individuality and enthusiasm with your writing and selling skills.

'Worthy every penny. If you're really serious about being published, this book should be your bible.' – *Writers' Bulletin*

'Really definitive … Leaves every other similar book in its shade"'– *National Poetry Foundation*

ISBN 1 85703 877 0

How To Books are available through all good bookshops, or you can order direct from us through Grantham Book Services:

Tel: +44 (0)1476 541080
Fax: +44 (0)1476 541061
Email: orders@gbs.tbs-ltd.co.uk.

Or via our website at www.howtobooks.co.uk.

To order via any of these methods, please quote the title(s) of the book(s) and your credit card number together with its expiry date.

For further information about our books and catalogue, please contact:

How To Books
3 Newtec Place
Magdalen Road
Oxford OX4 1RE.

Visit our web site at www.howtobooks.co.uk or contact us by email at info@howtobooks.co.uk.

Michael Oke and his colleagues assist in the writing of private life stories. Via a series of home visits, or by correspondence, guidance and encouragement is provided for those looking to write for family, friends and for the sheer fun of it.

Editing and production services are also offered to those who have already written a manuscript. Either way, the end result is a few high quality, leather-bound volumes, including photographs. Low runs of smaller hardback and paperback books can also be provided.

If you would like more information about Bound Biographies and the services they can provide, fill in your contact details here and return to the address below.

Name:

Address:

Phone:

Bound Biographies Ltd, 21 Heyford Park House
Heyford Park, Bicester, Oxon OX25 5HD
Telephone: 01869 232911
www.boundbiographies.com

Michael Oke and his colleagues assist in the writing of private life stories. Via a series of home visits, or by correspondence, guidance and encouragement is provided for those looking to write for family, friends and for the sheer fun of it.

Editing and production services are also offered to those who have already written a manuscript. Either way, the end result is a few high quality, leather-bound volumes, including photographs. Low runs of smaller hardback and paperback books can also be provided.

If you would like more information about Bound Biographies and the services they can provide, fill in your contact details here and return to the address below.

Name:

Address:

Phone:

Bound Biographies Ltd, 21 Heyford Park House
Heyford Park, Bicester, Oxon OX25 5HD
Telephone: 01869 232911
www.boundbiographies.com